Praise for:

Becoming
A Mean, Teen Parenting Machine

Parenting Machine gives specific tips to help parents gain greater understanding of, and empathy for, their teens—which is key to improving relationships. It also specifically addresses critical mental health issues that are devastating many of our youth. Parents are typically ill equipped to address these issues and Machine provides valuable guidance.

—**Jeff Dyer, Ph.D**, *professor, and author of the bestselling "The Innovator's DNA."*

***

Over the years, I've heard many a parent exclaim (when in the midst of a trying, difficult, or broken relationship with a teenager), "I've had it up to here"—and their flattened palm waves high overhead. I've come to think this comment misses the mark completely. More likely, they have run out of options. So, they keeping doing the same things over and over and expecting better results. In "Becoming a Mean, Teen Parenting Machine," Wirig provides numerous techniques, steps, actions, and strategies plus powerful explanations and examples to help parents build mutual trust, show love and not just say love, and deal with the challenges of technology, anxiety, withdrawal, and anger to name a few. When parents have more tools and options, they increase their odds of having a healthy relationship with their teens.

—**Al Switzler**- *Co-author of "Crucial Conversations" and Influencer*

As a parent of four children (two of them teenagers), and as a busy general pediatrician, I can absolutely relate to many parents out there who feel lost trying to be great parents to their teenagers. Whether it is trying to communicate effectively, or being fully present in those critical moments, or even just handling the roller-coaster of emotions that teens (and parents) often feel in trying to relate together, teenagers present many challenges for parents who are literally learning on the job. Despite these challenges, parenting teenagers can be extremely fun, and exciting. Adolescence is a time of deep social and emotional learning, a time of growth, a time of fascination with the world and finding one's place in it. All too often, in my experience, parents generally have their child's best interest at heart, but fail to fully embrace this complex, yet wonderful window in parenting time. We often fail to understand how to relate to or communicate with our teens. And then, even with that understanding, we often fail to know how to effectively implement meaningful change into our daily parenting. That is why this book is a must read for ALL parents and care-givers. This book very simply lets you in on those crucial parenting secrets, those pearls of wisdom that will allow you to transform your parenting, to unlock, to build and to magnify your relationship with your teenager. The step-by-step tools presented in this book will help you gain the knowledge and the confidence to shape and reshape your relationship with your teenager, grounded on a foundation of trust, love, understanding, communication and respect. I absolutely loved this book because the principles taught in it are so simple and yet so profound. Now, I just have to continue to work on implementing them into my own parenting!

—**Tyson Jones**, *M.D. Board Certified Pediatrician and father of four*

***

In today's busy and ever-changing world, there are many parents who feel uncertain, inadequate, or lost when it comes to raising teenagers. Having a *good* relationship with your teens can seem impossible.

Becoming a Mean Teen Parenting Machine can change that story for your family. The tools, resources, tips, and patterns Wirig shares are *game changers* for relationships with teens. Concepts like understanding each individual child, becoming aware of our interactions and conversations as a family, and tools to combat the plagues of emotional and mental illness are particularly significant for families today. Katie has beautifully woven practical strategies and mindset patterns into this book with a feeling of hope and joy, not shame and guilt.

This is a must-read for parents who want to have positive, long-lasting, and meaningful relationships with their children.

—**Katrina Seamons**, *Founder of Deliberatefamily.com @deliberatefamily, and mother of five.*

***

Working as a therapist with at-risk youth battling mental health issues, I realize the importance of strong families and a stable home life for them. I believe it is the hardest time in the history of mankind to be a parent. Because of this I believe that parents need a lot more resources to know how to support and connect with their kids. The Parenting Machine is such a tool. It gives parents actionable advice that, if followed, will ensure lasting results that will improve the quality of their relationships. As guardians, parents and educators implement the principles taught in this book we will see a change in the mental health of today's youth and a stronger resolve to repair and heal problems in the home.

—**Stuart Squires**, *LCSW, Youth Crisis Worker and father of eight.*

***

The Parenting Machine draws our attention to our most important relationships, the relationship we have in our homes and with our children. Every good parent wants more secure relationships with our teenage children, but we don't know how to get it. Wirig provides actionable ideas that when applied can profoundly impact the quality of our parenting, and will result in stronger, more secure and happier youth. If we want safer communities, including a decrease in violence, bullying, and depression, we have to first focus on our home life. It all starts in our homes and with us, the parents. This parenting guide should be on every bookshelf and referenced frequently by parents who desire a more peaceful and loving home.

—Timothy Ballard, *best-selling author of Slave Stealers, and founder of O.U.R: Operation Underground Railroad.*

Becoming a

Mean, Teen Parenting Machine

A step-by-step guide to transform your relationship with your teenager

Katie Millar Wirig, M.A.

Published by KHARIS PUBLISHING, an imprint of

KHARIS MEDIA LLC.

Copyright © 2023 Katie Millar Wirig, M.A.

ISBN-13: 978-1-63746-202-7

ISBN-10: 1-63746-202-6

Library of Congress Control Number: 2023930481

All KHARIS PUBLISHING products are available at special quantity
discounts for bulk purchase for sales promotions, premiums, fund-raising,
and educational needs. For details, contact:

Kharis Media LLC
Tel: 1-479-599-8657
support@kharispublishing.com
www.kharispublishing.com

Contents

Prologue

When my fifth and final child was born, my oldest was seven years old. You read that right, five children in seven years. At the time, I thought nothing could be harder than raising five small humans who were completely dependent on me for everything. A friend told me, "You think this is hard, wait until they grow up, one day you will have five teenagers." I laughed, thinking nothing could be harder than the baby stage. I was wrong.

The teenage and pre-teen years are some of the most rewarding times, but can also be incredibly challenging. It is like trying to solve a maze that is constantly changing. We think we've gone the right direction, then a wall moves, and we find ourselves lost once again. In the early years, my solution to the problem was to try and control the situation. I adopted a false belief that through my actions I would be able to control my children and their lives. I believed that if I kept my home as perfect as possible, I would produce perfect children. Unfortunately, kids are not math equations; one plus one doesn't always equal two. The outcome of our actions will depend on a variety of variables, many of them, out of our control. We can do everything "right" and our children may still struggle. This doesn't mean that we throw up our hands and give up. Instead, we strive for the ideal, knowing that the ideal is not attainable, but still worth the effort.

Rather than view parenting as an all-or-nothing principle, thinking that if we show our children love and give them clear boundaries, they will never participate in dangerous activities. We should look at it like drops in a bucket. Imagine that you need to fill a bucket with water. Some days you make great strides by placing a cup full of water in the bucket. On other days, it is only a couple of drops, but the important thing is that you are always filling it. Small drops add up. Eventually, the bucket will fill. Unfortunately, there may be times when our actions, or the actions of others, cause the bucket to spill a little or leak. In those cases, we patch up the hole and get back to filling it.

As a mental health coach I advise families to provide possible solutions to challenges in relationships. Years ago, while earning my credentials, I simply read and learned about parenting. I thought I would have all the answers when my time came to become a mother; I believed there was a fix to every problem. Real life has a way of forcing you to confront reality. Even all the education school could offer did not fully prepare me for the everyday challenges that parents face while raising fiercely independent and distinctive individuals. What I gained from my professional education was theories and possible plans to execute those theories. What I learned from parenting my own children are compassion and flexibility. Compassion for myself and other parents that I work with both professionally and personally. I discovered that even the best intentioned parents, including myself, will still have challenges in their homes. The once-know-it-all college student of years past has transformed into a mom of 5 rowdy teens, tweens, and toddlers, who embraces imperfections and welcomes the chaos. Although my education in the social sciences has been invaluable, the real learning takes place in the trenches with other parents doing the paramount work of raising children.

In this book, information will be presented in the "ideal" form. For instance, in the chapter on handling emotional outbursts, the parent is advised to be unemotional. This doesn't mean that the next time our child has an outburst and we don't handle it correctly, we should set aside everything we've learned. But if at that moment we can help them manage their emotions just 1% better than we did before, that is still 1% more water in the bucket. The ideal is worth trying for, and still worth pursuing. No one is implementing these principles 100% of the time. Yet, just because we can't be perfect, it does not mean that we give up trying. Our teens usually adopt an all-or-nothing mindset, as illustrated in the chapter about motivation. This belief sets them up for failure. Life is not all or nothing; it is marginal gains. Just as we advise our teens to keep trying and do their best, we should repeat that same mantra to ourselves. Take what is taught in this book and implement it in the most realistic way possible. Know that even when parents do everything "correctly" the child may not make the "correct" choice. Your child's actions are *not* in your control, but *your* actions are.

Throughout the book, you will read a variety of personal examples to illustrate principles. All of these examples are from clients from my work as a mental wellness coach and my personal experiences as a mother. Names have been changed to protect the privacy of the individuals, but the content remains true. Furthermore, this book was written not just for parents, but for grandparents, foster parents, educators, and anyone working with teenagers. The label of guardians, caregivers, and parents are used interchangeably. In addition, pre-teens and teenagers are referred to as youth, children, tweens, and teens throughout the book.

I desire that you will think of each of your children individually. See them for who they are, what they need, and how you can help them reach their potential. Then, when both of you fall short of being your best selves, pick each other up, wrap each other in a bear hug, and give each other a "do-over." A do-over is one of the kindest things you can give to another person. You acknowledge that you made a mistake. You assure them it can be forgiven and forgotten as long as you both have the desire to do better. Give yourself grace as you parent your children. Understand that every small change you make in your home will be another drop in the bucket. Know that you are putting them on a path to becoming a more successful, well-adjusted, and happy individual.

CHAPTER 1

Understanding Your Teen's Personality & Love Language

One of the first steps to creating a healthy and strong bond with your child is to fully understand their personality and how they feel loved. Think back to when you were a new parent; you may have felt like you had an alien on your hands. That tiny baby would cry at random times, and it was up to you to determine what the cry meant. Were they hungry? Tired? Teething? Just plain grouchy? Or all of the above? It was probably frustrating in those early days when you had to get to know your newborn and what their cues were. As you spent more time with your child, and as they grew a little older, you actually did get to know your baby. You knew what cry meant he was hungry, or that your daughter preferred bananas to sweet potatoes. To a stranger, it might have appeared that you were making it up. How could someone really know a baby? But you did. You knew your child and they knew you.

Understanding a baby and toddler may have felt difficult at the time, but you did succeed. Now, as you consider your teenager, you may wish they were as easy to crack as your toddler. Unpredictable behavior is the name of the game during adolescence. Something that worked well one day may not work the next. Their moods are unpredictable. They are constantly changing and discovering who they are.

Even though your child is going through a lot of changes and is experiencing a wide variety of mood swings, they are solidifying some of their personality traits. This is exciting for the parent. As your child's personality develops, you will see glimpses of what your adolescent may become as an adult. During this challenging, yet exciting time, it is important for you to study, get to know, and, most of all, validate and love your child.

There are a variety of books that categorize personalities. Each of these have different methods for grouping personality traits. Not everyone appreciates categorizing people. It may feel offensive to be put in some sort of group that describes their motivations, likes, dislikes, communication style, and more. However, these types of groupings can be incredibly helpful in understanding your loved ones. Consider Brandon's story:

Brandon was a father of six children. Parenting six was overwhelming to say the least. He was the primary breadwinner for their household. His wife, Brenda, was very capable, loving, and great with the kids. For the most part, he didn't need to worry about the day -to-day care and safety of his children. His main focus was to spend quality time with them: mentoring, teaching, and most of all, loving them. Four of his children were easy for Brandon. He found their hobbies, interests, and communication styles relatable. It was enjoyable for Brandon to spend time with these kids because they had shared interests. The time spent together was gratifying. However, he couldn't seem to understand his second oldest and youngest children. He would try to talk to them, but they would take it the wrong way; and, at times, it would become awkward or turn into a fight. Brandon didn't like personality tests. He felt claustrophobic when assigning himself and others groupings or categories. He generally avoided them. He was complaining to his wife that he couldn't seem to connect with these two children whom he loved dearly, but couldn't quite understand. Brenda suggested that he read a book about personality types, The Child Whisperer[1]. He reluctantly agreed. Although he didn't love everything about the book, Brandon admitted that the information was helpful in understanding each of his children better. He began implementing the things he learned in the book with his children, and he saw unprecedented results. He found it so helpful that he decided to seek out more personality tests. He even initiated a family activity where everyone in the family took the DiSC test[2]. They enjoyed a night going through each person's results, discussing the funny things that

---

[1] Tuttle, C. (2012) *The Child Whisperer*. Draper, UT: Live Your Truth Press

[2] Your Life's Path Consulting and Teambuilding, *Your Life's Path*, 2022, *Accessed September 2022*,
<*https://www.thediscpersonalitytest.com/?view=Assessments_disc&gclid=Cj0KCQjwguG YBhDRARIsAHgRm4-s5zqLq14ZnRXT-UMQONs7UnzEcMHamkye-YO_tZ1EwvS8okTRKoEaAuPgEALw_wc*>

made them tick, but also the things that made them special. As Brandon relayed to me, "The amazing thing about it was by focusing on each person and their test, they felt loved and valued. It was a great chance for them to express why they felt the way they did, why certain things bother them, and other things that made them feel happy. The test was a vehicle of communication, it gave them the words to say 'This is what I have been trying to say' because it helped each of us to express some of the more complex parts of our personalities. It was helpful to do it as a family. It gave all of us the chance to focus on each other better, to learn about each individual, discover ways to help them succeed, and make sure each person felt loved."

Brandon's experience is not uncommon. Many people are reluctant to try new things like personality tests or read books about personality. It feels overwhelming. Like Brandon, they might have opinions about categorizing people, so they avoid beneficial resources. There is great value gained when you truly understand your child. Lori Gottileb explained that when people come to therapy for family miscommunication, what they want from their loved ones is not only to be told, "I love you," but also "I *understand* you."[3]

It is a very isolating feeling to be misunderstood. Your teenager will feel secure in the relationship if you can show them that you understand them. One parent went above and beyond when she explained that as she nears the birthday of each child, she will re-read a personality book with that child in mind. Her goal is to better understand that child. She feels like this is the best gift she can give her children: the gift of understanding and acceptance. The gift of being able to communicate, "I love you just the way you are, and it is important to me that you feel understood and loved." Her children see and appreciate her efforts. She has built a bridge between herself and her children that shows she understands them and loves them. The

---

[3] Gottileb, L., (2019) *Maybe You Should Talk To Someone: A Therapist, Her Therapist, and Our Lives Revealed.* Boston: Houghton Mifflin Harcourt

result is her children are confident, happy, and secure in their relationships.

A great thing about adolescence compared to toddlerhood is that your teenager's personality is solidifying. In the early days of parenting, you probably didn't have a lot of information about who your child was. Their likes and dislikes were constantly changing, but each year they would become a little more secure in their interests. By the time the child is around 18-24, you will see their fully developed personality. Although the young adult is still growing and changing, the majority of their personality is fully formed. Those years leading up to adulthood will display very clearly what their main motivations are, their preferred style of communication, if they are extroverted or introverted, and so much more.

Love Languages

Understanding your child's core personality, their motivations, and the things that make them tick are all important. In addition, it is essential to explore the way they feel loved. One of the most well-known and helpful books on this topic is: *The 5 Love Languages*, written by Gary Chapman[4]. Chapman has helped many couples find healing in their relationships by exploring better ways to express love and feel loved. The premise of the book is that there are five ways you can show or feel love: service, gifts, words of affirmation, touch, and quality time. Most people show love within one of these five ways. It is interesting to note that we might show love one way but feel loved another. As Dr. Chapman explains, many people feel unloved in their relationships, not because they are *actually unloved*; but because their partner is expressing love in a way they don't feel. Perhaps a husband shows love by giving service. He cleans the car, makes his wife's favorite foods, or completes some of her chores throughout the day. His wife doesn't appreciate all these acts of service, nor does she feel loved this way. Instead, she wants more physical touch. She desires hand holding,

---

[4] Chapman, Gary D. (2010). *The Five Love Languages*. Farmington Hills, Mi: Walker Large Print.

sitting close on the couch, a back rub, and hugs given freely and often. The husband, who isn't comfortable with physical connection, rarely touches his wife outside of the privacy of their bedroom. His wife feels unloved, and the husband is completely baffled as to why because he is *constantly* showing love. This is a common problem for many. In couples' therapy, often the therapist first will address if the couple knows each other's love languages; and second if they are doing what they can to express love in a way their partner can feel it.

This principle applies to children as well. A common insecurity of teenagers is that they feel they don't fit in. This might be the most prevalent problem with today's youth: the feeling that something is wrong with them, and that they don't have a place to belong. Our teenagers are so insecure about being loved and accepted that most behavior problems stem from this insecurity. Parents have a lot of power. Even though teenagers are branching out and are likely giving more credence to their peers than they are to parents, the home is the foundation of their self-esteem and feelings of self-worth. If they know they are loved dearly and unconditionally at home, they will have a stronger sense of self-worth with their peers. Unfortunately, many of us don't take the time to genuinely get to know each individual child to determine what they need to feel loved by us. Often parents choose one method that seemingly works and stick to it with every child. The danger is that every kid is different and unique. This is why four children can grow up in the same home, with the same environment and same parenting style; and one will go North, the other South, the other two East, and West. Parents scratch their heads and wonder how each of their kids perceived their childhood so differently. I am not suggesting that we completely overhaul our parenting style for each child, but I am proposing that time be taken for each child to discover how they feel loved. Then we can put forth more effort to show them love in a way that our children can fully receive it. Here are some examples of what each type of love language could look like.

Service

We are serving our families all the time. Much of our lives can feel like we are slaves to the most basic needs of our children. This is a way parents show love every moment of every day. Unfortunately, doing something like the laundry may not help them feel loved because, tragically, it is now an expectation that mom or dad will just do their laundry.

There are two things caregivers can do to show love through service, even though they are already serving them all the time. The first is to lovingly point out all the things that we are doing for them. Don't do it in a way that suggests that they owe you, or that it is nagging. If it is said every five minutes, "look, I am picking up your shoes" or "I did your laundry today," it will create an unhealthy balance of feeling like the kid is always indebted. Instead, kindly point out things that you are doing, and follow it with something like "I decided to make your favorite meal tonight because I wanted you to know I was thinking about you." When you point out what you are doing, make sure you say it in a way that makes them feel loved, not in debt.

Second, do a little extra for this certain child. For example, it is a chore day, and everyone is doing their chores. Your teen had a bad day yesterday and is feeling sorry for themselves. You could say, "I can finish the last of your chore so you can go relax. I know you had a hard day yesterday. Why don't you take a little time for yourself and come join us when you are ready?" Imagine how that would feel to your child. They would not only feel loved, but they would feel seen and heard. That type of compassion creates a strong bond between a parent and the child. They know that their parents are aware of them and their needs.

Gifts

In a world where our children are already spoiled, this can be a hard one for many parents to wrap their heads around. They might not like the idea of giving their children too many gifts, especially if each gift needs to be something big and expensive. Frequent expensive gifts are an unrealistic way to show love. However, if they feel loved through gifts, it is less about the size of the gift and more about believing that someone loves them enough to sacrifice for them. For example, I have a child who feels loved through gifts. It has little to do with the gift being expensive; instead, he is so flattered when he knows that I was thinking about him when I wasn't with him. He adores it when I go to the grocery store and surprise him with a bag of chips or a snack that he loves. When I get home, I might hand him a small bag of beef jerky with a wink and he practically blushes with delight. He knows that mom was thinking about him and loves him! Another gift that makes a big impact for this child are pictures. I would print out a picture and write on the back, "this day was so fun!" Or, "you look so handsome in this picture." Then I would leave it on his bed. I initially thought it was a silly idea, but I learned that he has kept all these pictures in a little box under his bed. At times I catch him looking at the pictures. These small gifts cost me almost nothing, but they speak volumes to this son who needs to know that he is on my mind.

Words of Affirmation

Children who feel loved with words of affirmation are the kids who live for praise and compliments. They love it when parents and friends point out things that are good about them. They might even do things that are seemingly annoying to try to get you to acknowledge them. These are the kids that say, "Mom, watch this!" Or, "Look at my homework" when they know they did a good job. For many parents, this type of exaggerated compliment fishing can be hard. It might actually make you feel like you don't want to compliment them because they are fishing for praise too much. When your child is fishing, try not to get frustrated; instead, try to view it as your child needing extra validation and love.

These kids thrive when they are complimented and directly told they are loved. Compliments and expressions of love are vital to these children, additionally many of these kids also benefit from conversations where they are validated. They need to process everything by talking it out. At times it might feel exhausting, especially if this is not the parents' love language. The parent might feel like they are validating the child all the time. Many times, after you open the door with a compliment or praise, the child might jump into a ten minute story about their day. If this is your child, your goal is to listen and validate. This is how their self-esteem is fostered and how they will feel loved by their parents.

Touch

Touch is vital to your child's development and well-being. As a result, there is an entire chapter dedicated to the power of physical touch for your child. If your child feels loved through touch, look for creative ways throughout the day to give them all the physical affection that they need. Refer to Chapter 9 for more ideas.

Quality Time

Quality time is one of the best ways parents can show love to their children of any age. Although there are some individuals who primarily feel loved through quality time, this is something that all parents should be doing with their children often, even if it isn't their preferred love language. In fact, through spending quality time together, parents will determine their child's love language and take inventory of how the relationship is thriving and where it could improve.

There are a couple of different ways to spend quality time together. For those in big families, group outings are a great option. The goal is to ensure that the parent is mentally present and living in the moment. This can be one of the biggest challenges for busy parents. In a world that is increasingly vying for our attention, both children and adults are often distracted. When we are working, we are often distracted with thoughts of play, household duties, and daydreaming. Conversely, when we are spending time with family, we are often distracted with work. It is a vicious cycle that causes us to be unable to fully commit to anything. Something that all of us could benefit from is learning how to be present and give our full attention to whatever it is we are doing. If you are hiking with your child, be present in the moment. Listen to the conversation, look around at the beautiful surroundings, and breathe deeply the fresh air. When you are working, force your mind to think about your professional duties and set aside the longing feeling that you need to be elsewhere. If we are fully present in each situation, we will find that our time becomes more productive. We actually feel less guilt for not doing something else. This is the key to quality time with children: be present both physically and mentally. Help them to feel like their parents are truly there with them and don't want to be anywhere else.

Here is Jim's experience:

Being present was a hard implementation for Jim. Even though he knew he needed to be more present it wasn't natural for him. He was a distracted child and it followed him into adulthood. As an adult, he was no longer rowdy or overly talkative, but he found that he had a hard time giving his full attention to whatever he was doing. He felt like he was always looking forward. If he was doing one thing, he was thinking about the next thing. He often experienced feelings of guilt that he wasn't doing something else. Eventually, Jim started to see problems arise with his teenage children as their relationships started to suffer. Though he was spending time with his children, at least by the clock, his children would complain that he wasn't genuinely there. Their perception was that he didn't enjoy time with them. While together, Jim would be on his phone answering work calls or be in deep thought. While the kids talked to him, he would only pick up bits and pieces of what they were saying. This was because: 1) he wasn't that interested in what they were saying, and 2) he had so much on his plate that listening to his kid talk about NFL football highlights seemed like a waste of time. He felt his brain power needed to be spent on things that were really important, like solving a complicated issue at work. After learning that he was only spending *time* with his family but not *quality time*, Jim decided to make some changes. Since it was really hard for him to separate himself from work and other duties, he decided to try doing small getaways where he felt like he could unplug.

This stemmed from him perceiving that when they were on a family vacation, he was a totally different person. He turned off work notifications, he lived in the moment, and his family expressed that they loved "vacation Dad." He chose to implement "vacation Dad" in small ways. For instance, he offered to take his sons fishing. While fishing, he tried to turn his "work mind" off like he would if he were in vacation mode. For those five precious hours that they fished, he shut off notifications to his phone, told himself beforehand that there was nothing he could do to solve a work problem now, and promised himself he would be mentally present with his boys. The payoff was startling. He worried that he would need to put in hours to make his kids feel special. He thought it would take days to break through the surface pleasantries with a son who was more reserved, but this was not the case. His boys responded quickly. The benefit of those five hours far exceeded the amount of time that was put in. This is the benefit of spending quality time together. It really is about the quality, not only about the quantity. Five good hours spent together can be more beneficial than a week of distracted parenting.

For most parents, the obstacle to quality time is just that, the time. We have busied ourselves so much that trying to find a couple of hours in the week to spend with our children can feel nearly impossible; not to mention, if you want to spend time with each child individually. Between juggling the child and the parents' schedule, it may seem like there is just no way. The benefits are so abundant, however, that this is a place where we cannot fail. It might mean that children opt out of extracurricular activities or parents decline a work project. Also, don't underestimate making better use of the time we already have. For example, each time you drive your child back and forth from a sporting event can be quality time. If you can be present during that drive, talking with your child, enjoying the music, playing a trivia game, etc, you can make the 30-minute drive into quality time. Parents often miss opportunities with their children that are spent with the child on their phone, the parent distracted, or both parties lost in their own thoughts.

The important thing to take away from this is that we can make all the time we spend together more meaningful. There is time if we look for it. It is how we spend time that will determine if it enhances familial relationships.

It All Starts in The Home

There are a variety of ways to show children just how much we love them. The lasting effects of a child who feels fully and deeply loved are unmeasurable. Society as a whole has so many problems: hate, violence, crime, depression, suicide, and so much more. There are many well-meaning people who try to solve the problems from the top down. This might be by creating more programs implemented by national leaders in attempts to address these problems. We should do everything we can to address it on a national and global level; but, as many of us have already realized, when you enhance the most basic familial and meaningful relationships in people's lives, the outcome is less hate, violence, depression, etc. It won't solve everything wrong in society, but it will certainly make a massive difference.

Parents have more power through showing love than we ever thought possible. Helping others feel loved, wanted, and like they belong, can be the springboard that teens need to propel them towards successful adulthood. As they head into their adult lives, they will bring change to their communities. Your children, feeling loved and wanted, will treat their peers at school with love and respect. This will encourage other students to do same, and communities will become stronger.

All of this love has to happen in the home. It has to happen with those who first loved them: caregivers, parents, grandparents, and guardians. If we want to make real changes in our communities and in society as a whole, we have to be willing to make some of the hardest changes inside our own home. We must learn how to show compassion and patience, even when we are tired. We must take the time to learn how to best love our children, even when we don't feel especially loved in return. We can have a massive impact on the future by simply loving and understanding those in our own homes.

CHAPTER 2

Building A Foundation of Trust

Trust is the foundation of every good relationship. Even though we know this, it is a challenge to take the time and effort to build it. Rarely do we trust someone the moment we meet them. Instead, we need time to get to know them. We need to have experiences with them where they prove themselves. Then, over time, they earn our trust. Each instance we interact with someone we either gain or lose trust. If the interactions are positive, a foundation of trust is built. If the interactions are negative, feelings of betrayal, doubt, or weariness prevail. This is same with teenagers. Parents build trust with their children during their adolescent years. Children are given more independence. Their actions with that independence will determine if they will earn more freedom and privileges in the future.

When children are little, parents can get away with saying "because I said so" when the child couldn't have or do something they wanted. Many times the child would stomp away angrily, but still avoided doing the thing they were told not to do. When they are young, parents can discipline a child quite easily. If they don't obey, mom could physically restrain or put them in time out. If they talk back, dad could take away playing with friends or having a treat. Parents have complete control over their child's environment; obeying parents is a way of survival. Without you, your young child quite simply wouldn't have survived, and they know it. You are an emotional rock for your young child, but you are also their physical rock and their very life depends on you providing for them.

As children get older and more independent, they depend on their parents for survival less and less. This is a good thing. We all hope as our children age that they will be able to survive in the world alone, and that they will have the skills needed to take care of themselves. However, this also means that they have resources to get what they want, even if their parents aren't the ones to give it to them. For example, a guardian might take away dessert from a middle school child. So they use the cash they have from babysitting to go to the vending machine and get a sweet treat. A parent grounds their

teenager. So they sneak out. Unfortunately, the child is physically too strong for the parent to wrestle them into staying. During adolescence, the consequences parents impose will be less immediate and more long-term. The consequence will have more to do with the approval of their caregiver rather than an actually imposed punishment. Trust is the way we get a child to follow the rules when they are too old to impose immediate consequences.

Many times we think of trust with our teenage children as a one-way street; they need to earn our trust, not the other way around. Some parents think of this exchange as a teenager earning *a parent's* trust. The teenager behaves well; the parent trusts the teen. Consequently, the teen gets more privileges. Equally important, however, is how much the teen trusts the parents. Trust is a fluid thing between two individuals. When a child trusts a parent, they know that their parent is an honest, loving, and dependable person. When a parent trusts a child, the parent knows that the child will do what they agreed to do. The benefit of this exchange is that a teenager is more likely to listen to counsel and obey warnings from people that they trust.

Trust works differently than discipline. It is preventative, not reactive. A healthy, trusting relationship between parent and child will prevent certain behaviors from happening. The definition of trust is the "firm belief in the reliability, truth, ability, or strength of someone or something."[5] Does your child have a firm belief that what you are saying is true? When you tell them that if they get poor grades they will lose opportunities for their future career, do they believe you? When you explain that engaging in dangerous activities like underage drinking or drug use will harm the very biology of their brain, do they trust that what you are saying is true? Does your child *believe* you? Does he believe that when you tell them to do something or not to do something you are telling them because the consequences are actually dangerous? Or

---

[5] Oxford Learner's Dictionary 2022, *Definition of Trust,* Oxford University Press, Accessed August 2022,
    <www.oxfordlearnersdictionaries.com/us/definition/english/trust_2>

do they believe you are simply trying to control them through scare tactics?

Think of the people you trust most. These relationships have been built on past experience together where the person has said something that has proven to be true. Thus, in the future, you believe them. Consider this oversimplified scenario: you are told by an acquaintance who is rude and overdramatic that you are talking too much during a work meeting. Initially, you are offended, yet also worried they may be right. After further thought, you decide this person doesn't know you and you choose to ignore the comment. You continue acting the way you always have and roll your eyes whenever this person makes a comment during a meeting. Conversely, consider this: you are at a work party with your best friend. After observing you for a while, your friend kindly lets you know that you are talking too much and that you could try listening more. Once again, you might be a little offended and embarrassed. After giving it some thought, you choose to follow your friend's advice. You truly *believe* that this friend only wants the best for you. You believe that they wouldn't have said something unless it was *true*. You have a relationship that is built on trust. This friend doesn't lie to you. They tell you things to help you. This is the type of relationship we should strive to have with our teenage children.

Our interactions with our teenagers and how much they trust us will directly impact the way that they take our criticisms, help, and encouragement to follow the rules. If we have built the relationship on intimidation or using cheap tactics to simply control them, they will see right through it. They might not have noticed it when they were kids, but they will surely see it when they are teenagers. They will recognize when they are being controlled, and they will rebel; strictly because they want to prove they can't be restricted. The goal is to develop a relationship that is built on mutual trust. When they know their parents are trustworthy, they will follow the rules because they know it will translate to more privileges and independence. They will also believe that their guardian has their best interest at heart.

The first key to building a loving and trusting relationship with teenagers is to start small. Parents must prove that they are a person of their word and that the things that they say come to fruition. For example, if your child asks for a late night, and you agree on the condition that they mow the lawn first, you need to follow through. In the beginning, you may need to point out the reason for their reward. It might sound silly, but you should say, "thank you for mowing the lawn, you did something for me, and now I am happy to do something for you. Plan that late night with your friends and I will take everyone home when it is done." This kind of arrangement empowers your child. They now feel like they have control of the situation. They can barter for the things that they want. They know that if they follow through on their end, you will follow through on yours. Conversely, consider this example. The child mows the lawn with the promise of a late night. After they mow the lawn, you change your mind, seemingly tricking them by saying, "you should mow the lawn because you live in my house. Maybe we can find a different day to do a late night, but not today." You have now damaged the relationship. You have effectively told them their actions aren't directly related to the outcome of their lives. This doesn't necessarily mean that every job has to be tied to some privilege. There are many jobs they should do simply because they live in your house. The difference here is that you had communicated with them what the outcome would be from completing a chore. When they fulfill their end of the deal, you have to fulfill yours. This will build trust.

As parents start with small acts to build trust, the child will start to connect dots in their mind. They will see how their actions affect their lives. Caregivers should directly point out ways that the child's actions have impacted the consequences. When they win a reward at school, draw the parallel of hard work to reward by saying, "I am so proud of all those hours you put in practicing and listening to your coaches; your hard work has paid off." These small statements will show them that all things in life come as a result of something else. They need to clearly see that their actions affect the outcome.

31

Consider Jake's experience with his son, Mason. Mason was a difficult child and was constantly doing things that made their family life hard. Even though Mason was the reason for much of the family discord, he saw himself as a victim. He was continually blaming everyone else for his problems. If he wasn't able to go to a friend's house, it was because his parents loved his siblings more than they loved Mason. If he couldn't get a new pair of shoes, he felt deprived of the things he felt he deserved. He continually disobeyed his parents when they would try to discipline him. Mason would respond by saying, "nothing I do matters, you are just trying to control me and punish me." This was frustrating for Jake. Mason desired more independence and trust, but he hadn't earned it. Jake was being blamed for it.

After some counseling, Jake decided to try something different with Mason. He set up a strict family economy where everyone could essentially "buy" privileges. In the past, Jake and his wife would pay for everything and believed themselves to be loving parents by taking care of all the family expenses. They perceived that for Mason, it might help him to understand the scarcity of money and the *why* behind purchases, time with friends, family vacations, etc. They implemented a new system where Mason would earn money for things that he did. He would be given an allowance of both time and money; money to buy things, and time accrued to trade in for time with friends and outings. This allowance depended on good behavior and doing his jobs around the house. The catch was that Mason now had to pay for his own expenses. He also had to use accrued time allotments to do things with friends and to be driven to places. No longer would mom and dad cover clothing, outings with friends, or anything extra. He had a strict budget for school clothes. He had to pay for anything else he wanted. He was also given only a certain amount for extracurricular activities; and, once again, he had to cover any difference. His parents worried this would break Mason, but it actually empowered him! He was in control. Even though he had less money than he had when mom and dad were doing everything, he felt accountable and independent. If he wanted a new pair of shoes, he could buy them himself. If he wanted extra privileges, he could "buy" them from his parents. Because he had to budget his time and money, he no longer felt like his dad was controlling him. If he couldn't buy a new pair of shoes, he knew why and didn't blame it on his dad. If Mason wasn't able to be driven somewhere, he understood it was because he needed to earn it first. Over time, Mason let go of his victim mentality and became a happier and more responsible child. What Mason really wanted was to feel in control. This new family economy allowed him to feel empowered. As Jake held up his end and honored the system, trust was built. With this new arrangement, one person wasn't more in control than the other. Their relationship started to heal.

Initially, this may not seem like an exercise in trust, but this is exactly what it is. Mason had lost trust in his father that his father would follow through. He felt like the victim because his dad was in charge of everything in his life. When Jake didn't follow through the way Mason thought he should, Mason believed that he no longer had control. Rather than do what his father asked, he would be defiant just to get control. With this new system, Jake was able to show Mason that he could trust him. As Jake relinquished some control and gave Mason opportunities to be independent, they could begin trusting each other.

The second step is to follow the rules yourself. Building trust goes both ways. Our teenagers want to be trusted by us, and we want our teens to trust us enough to believe that we have their best interest at heart. This starts by being a person of integrity and a person of your word. No one is more skilled at recognizing hypocrisy than a teenage child. In fact, they may even find hypocrisy in the tiniest infraction. For instance, as a family, you may decide to put more restrictions on cell phone usage. After explaining to your son that social media accounts and cell phone games will be suspended for a month, only calls and texting will be permitted, be ready for him to police you. Every time you pull out your phone to even check a recipe on the internet, he will be there watching you. He may even make a snarky remark. Don't let this discourage you or cause you to abandon your plan. Instead, let this help you to learn how to handle criticism gracefully and allow this to be a learning experience for both of you. If the child is being disrespectful, that would need to be addressed. If they are simply pointing out, "you're using *your* cellphone" then you could respond with something like, "You're right, thanks for reminding me. We all need reminders." Or "Yep, you're right. I am just checking a recipe for dinner; you are welcome to come and look if you'd like." These sorts of statements tell our teenagers that we are holding ourselves to the same standard of excellence. We wouldn't ask them to do something that we're not willing to do ourselves. When our children, young or old, see us following rules, being transparent in our actions, and gracefully accepting reminders to be better, it paves the way for them to trust us.

You will find that as parents focus on building trust with their children it will pour into other aspects of their lives. Caregivers might notice their teenagers' improvement in their relationship with teachers at school or their boss at work. The teen will crave that type of trusting relationship with other people in their life. They might start to treat their boss at work differently; going above and beyond what is asked and soon becoming a favorite employee. They have learned that privileges, promotions, and strong relationships are built on interactions that facilitate trust. Hopefully, they will recognize that following the rules at school, listening to their teachers, and following moral leaders will bring them the most satisfaction and happiness. They will look for people of integrity who are trustworthy and they will emulate them.

A concern comes when the teenager builds this trusted relationship with friends or influences that would harm them. Gang violence, group think, and negative peer pressure stem from a toxic relationship where the child has misplaced their trust in someone or some dangerous group. Be mindful of this and keep a close eye out for your teen hitching their wagon to dangerous groups of friends. If your child has already immersed themselves with a dangerous friend group, or does in the future, know that it can be hard to break. They have built a sense of trust with the group. They might feel more "understood" by them than they do by their parents. This is the parent's cue to really put time and energy into cultivating a positive relationship with their child. If the parent tells their child they can't be with their group of friends anymore, it will likely backfire. They will most likely reject this statement. They feel a sense of belonging and trust with these friends. Instead, rather than tear them away from this group, *replace* the group. Guardians might not be able to find a friend group to replace it, but they can find a sports team, church class, music group (choir, orchestra, band), or even a community organization to keep them busy while the parent tries to build a stronger relationship with their teenager. Replacing a friend group can be very hard. While extracurricular activities can provide entertainment to keep the teen busy and away from the destructive peer group, the parent's job is to jump in and become a trusted ally to them. This doesn't mean that a parent becomes their "friend" and is no longer the parent. They are still very much their parents, but they can also be a welcomed companion. Future chapters will teach how to start conversations and find common interests that can build the relationship. Many times the teen is acting out with friends because they crave a sense of belonging that they aren't finding elsewhere. If parents work to create a safe space in the home, they will begin to lay a new foundation for a relationship built on trust and mutual respect.

CHAPTER 3

The Power of Positive Interactions

For most caregivers reading this book, the end goal is a more positive relationship with their teenager. Some readers are in a good place and want to keep it that way. These principles will help to do that. For some parents, the relationship with their teenage children is struggling. Toddlers tell parents how much they love them. They come to their guardians for comfort when they have a bad day. When they have a good day, mom or dad is the person they are most excited to see. Parents share in their joy and their pain. They are constantly needed and openly loved by their children. As a child ages, they naturally begin to pull away from their parents, especially if they crave more independence. Luckily, it is possible for teenage children to gain more independence and still maintain a positive relationship with their caregivers. The goal is to intentionally facilitate as many positive interactions with each other as possible.

As a child ages, parents become less of a participant in their lives and more of a spectator on the sidelines. Often, when a caregiver does get a chance to become involved, they only get time for a few quick suggestions before the teen ignores them and goes back to their lives. We see the mistakes our children make, and we watch them test boundaries. Our first instinct might be to take those few interactions and make sure that we are correcting their bad behavior. Surely that is a parent's job. It is expected that we will correct areas where they need to change. However, if every interaction they have with their parents is negative, it is not only damaging to the relationship but also damaging to their inner voice.

A person's inner voice is the voice that talks to them throughout the day. It is the voice they hear when they are nervous, when they make an embarrassing mistake, or when they are rejected by friends. This voice tells them who they are. Our teenager's inner voice will largely be created by us. For most people, their parents' voices are what they hear as they transition from adolescence into adulthood. If the majority of interactions with caregivers are critical and negative, it is practically guaranteed that the growing child's thoughts will turn towards the negative.

A loving caregiver would never desire for their child's inner voice to be negative. They are heartbroken when they learn that they might have played a role in their child not feeling confident about themselves. The good news is that parents have a massive impact on helping children create a more positive inner voice. This solidifies that our relationship with our children is a place of safety, love, and acceptance.

The 5:1 Ratio

In almost all interactions with a child, a parent should adopt a 5:1 ratio of five positive interactions to every one negative interaction. If a child is defiant and disrespectful, needs a lot of active parenting, or is just challenging to be around, 5:1 may seem impossible. Think back to the interactions you had with your child in the last 24 hours. How many times did you correct them, raise your voice, get annoyed, or authoritatively tell them what to do? Probably quite a few, let's say five times. As an example:

1.   They were late, and you had to nag them to move faster.

2.   During school hours, you saw an alert on your phone notifying you that your child was posting on social media while they were supposed to be focusing in class. Naturally, you sent them a message telling them to get off their phone.

3.   After they got home from school you asked them to unload the dishwasher and had to nag them to complete it.

4.   When they lost their temper at their sister, you lost your temper with both of them.

5.   Finally, at the dinner table when you tried to have a family dinner, they were yet again on their phone and you had to remind them to put the phone down.

These are very normal interactions with a teenager; all are behaviors you should address. Parents have to keep them on track with school, home chores, treating siblings kindly, and sticking to a schedule.

Children need to be corrected. They need those boundaries, and you are there to help them learn healthy boundaries.

Now, consider how many positive interactions you had with your child. This could be a loving touch, a compliment, a conversation where you listened, gave praise, or did an act of service for them. My guess is you maybe had five throughout the entire day, but it is likely less than that. As our days get busier, we tend to focus on the necessities. Many times the things seen as vital are nagging, yelling, policing, etc. Parents forget that helping children feel comfortable and loved is as important as keeping our children on track. If a teenager feels safe, loved, and valued, they will likely put their phone down at the dinner table and participate with the family. Not because they are forced to, but because they want to. They now feel like their opinions and time are valued by their parents and siblings. This is the benefit of flooding your child's life with at least 5 positive interactions for every 1 negative interaction. Some professionals even recommend as many as a 10 to 1 ratio, and you can work up to that, but start with 5 to 1.

In the beginning, you may find that you have to keep track of how many connections you have because it is a new concept. You will be surprised to see how many times you are reacting negatively to your child and then have to wrack your brain to find five positive things. Luckily, those five positive interactions will be easier and simpler than you think. Here are some suggestions:

Touch

Touch is one of the easiest ways to have a positive interaction with your child. It doesn't have to be a big hug, although hugs are great. You could gently rub them on the back when they walk by. For example, you are on your way to the fridge and they are sitting at the table; just brush your hand across their back lovingly. This shows them that they are seen, appreciated, and loved. You could randomly squeeze their hand and look them in the eye with a smile or perhaps a side hug after dinner. Sit close on the couch and let your shoulders touch. When they talk to you, place your hand on their arm, not in a controlling way, but in a loving and gentle way. These are all simple interactions that are positive and show that you love them and you *want* to be close to them.

Some families are not comfortable with touch. Chapter 9 dedicates a whole chapter to the importance of touch for your teenager. If this is a place of discomfort for you, work on yourself first and start with baby steps in implementing positive, healthy touch into your parent-child relationship.

Positive Words and Compliments

Saying something nice is a simple way to interact with your teen. Don't overthink it. Observations as innocent as "your hair is cute today," "I like those shoes with that outfit," etc. are very easy. You can point out something about their physical appearance that is pleasing or point out something different they did. For example: "you changed your hair today, I like it!" Another great idea is to simply state, "I am proud of you." It doesn't have to be a big gushing moment, just an acknowledgment that you are proud of who they are. Point out things they are good at. If they are good at a certain subject in school, say it. Don't be afraid to voice every good thought you have about your child in your head. Bringing up positive memories can also be fun. Like saying, "remember that ice cream place we went to when we visited the national park, that was so fun!"

Service

You serve your child every day; in fact, the majority of your life is spent in their service. They probably often don't appreciate it or say thank you. You are already serving your kid, but you can enhance your service. You can let them know that the things you are already doing to serve them are acts of love. Note: it is important that you don't make it seem like a quid pro quo. You shouldn't say, "I packed your lunch today, I hope that means that you will help me with dinner tonight." Instead say, "I know you were tired because you stayed up late doing homework, so I packed your lunch for you." You can also say, "I washed your shoes because I know it bothered you how dirty they got," etc. Sometimes when my kids ask me to do things above and beyond, like drive a group of friends to the movie theater, I will say, "Sure, but it is only because I really like you." This is a reminder that I am doing it out of love. Yes, they roll their eyes, but they also recognize it.

Little Gifts

We live in a world where our children and teenagers are often quite spoiled with material things and gifts. Most of us probably need to simplify our gift-giving more than we should increase it. We don't want our children's feelings of love or worth to be tied to material things. This one should be used sparingly. However, some children really feel loved through gift-giving. This might be because the act of giving a gift shows the person that when you are not with them, you are thinking of them. It also shows that you are willing to take the time, effort, and money to get something for the person. This gift might be their favorite candy, some snack crackers they enjoy, a small note left on their pillow at night, a t-shirt you knew they would like, or even a new tube of chapstick or lip gloss, etc. The goal in giving the gift is to make the child feel *seen* and *loved*. Too many teenagers believe themselves to be invisible to their parents and to the people around them. They want to be seen for who they are. If you have a child who is hard to crack, try giving some small gifts to see if they appreciate the gesture.

Simple Statements of Love

An easy and simple way to show love is to just say it. Get in the habit of saying, "love you," even on the go. If you don't feel comfortable with "I love you" you can try other statements that mean you love them without saying it directly like, "you're the best!" "You rock!" etc. Generally, statements of advice don't count towards the 5:1 positive interactions rule. Declarations such as "don't do anything I wouldn't do," "remember who you are," or "be good" might not count as positive. You don't know if the child will process it as a gesture of love or as a correction to something they are doing. They may find comfort in the statement and know it is coming from love, or they could see it as another reminder that they need to be better. In general, keep the statements simple and with no strings attached.

Here is an example of how one mother implemented this principle and saw extraordinary results: Jill was a seasoned mom of four kids. They were well-behaved, respectful, and motivated, that is, all but one child. Her middle child, Samuel, was just cut from a different cloth than the rest of the kids. He was angry, defiant, and craved his independence more than his parents' approval. If Jill asked him to go one way, he would choose the other simply to show that he was his own person. His defiance and desire to be different from the rest of the family was putting a strain on his and Jill's relationship. She felt like the majority of the time she was tiptoeing around him. In the beginning, when the behavior started to deteriorate, she resorted to correcting him. Now, because of his explosions of anger or defiance toward her, she had practically completely given up communicating with Samuel in fear of his reaction. After being coached on some possible solutions that all felt overwhelming, she finally decided to start with the 5:1 ratio and build a foundation with Samuel on positive interactions. It worked miracles for their family. Jill, always the overachiever, decided rather than wait to do a positive interaction after a negative one, she would start the morning ahead. Almost like a bank account where she would save up for a rainy day. Here is what a morning would look like for Jill when they started the positive interactions.

Samuel comes downstairs for school.

Jill: Good morning sweetheart, did you sleep well? (Pet names and interest in his comfort)

Samuel: *Grunts.* Not really!

Jill: Dang! Sorry! I decided to make your lunch because it looked like you were tired, and I wanted you to have a little extra time to sleep in. (Service)

Samuel: *disinterested* Thanks.

Jill: Would you like me to get you your breakfast? I would be happy to! (Service)

Samuel: Uh, sure.

Jill: *As she walks by him to get the cereal, she brushes her hand on his back and gives him an encouraging pat.* (positive touch)

Jill: I looked at your homework last night, you did a great job! I am really proud of you! (Compliments)

Samuel: Thanks.

Jill: Heads up, after school I will be gone so when you get home I won't be here. I am hoping that you can just stay here for an hour till I get home to make sure your younger brother doesn't come home to an empty house. (An ask, which could become a negative interaction if it goes poorly)

Samuel: Yeah, that's fine, I can stay here till 5:00.

Jill: Thank you! That's a big help. (Simple thanks when they do something good)

Jill chooses to be positive with Samuel in the morning so that they can start the day right. Here is what a morning like this would usually look like.

Jill: There you finally are! You are going to be late, what took you so long?

Samuel: I had a bad night and didn't want to wake up.

Jill: We all have bad nights, you have to learn to wake up on time. Did you make your lunch?

Samuel: No.

Jill: You know you are supposed to make it the night before. I'm always saying, if you would think ahead and prepare, we wouldn't be scrambling in the morning.

Samuel: I don't care, I just won't eat if it's that big of a deal.

44

Jill: Well you should at least get breakfast.

Samuel: I am not hungry.

Jill: There is no way you are going to school on an empty stomach and then having no lunch. I will just get it for you.

Samuel: I said I'm not hungry.

Jill: There is no way you aren't hungry, and if you aren't hungry now, you will for sure be starving later. *She gets the cereal which he won't eat to prove a point.*

Jill: By the way, I looked at your homework last night. It was done, which is good. See what I told you, doing it at night will make it easier in the morning. (I told you so)

Samuel: Whatever.

Jill: I need you to be home right after school, no going to friends, no staying after, I will be gone till five and your brother will be home alone. I expect you to be nice to him until I get back, are we clear?

Samuel: Why can't he stay by himself? He is old enough and I have other things I want to do. (fight starts)

Notice the difference between the two interactions. The second experience may be the one many caregivers often have with their teenagers. Notice how Jill is constantly putting Samuel on the defensive by starting their conversations with negative interactions. If parents have a child who is sensitive and desires more independence (which most teenagers do), they will be picking a fight the whole time. Making the interactions positive doesn't change the morning much. They still talked about packing lunches, breakfast, homework, and babysitting a younger sibling; but the outcome was extremely different. It also made Samuel feel like a loved and valued member of the family, rather than an annoyance to his mom.

After just 6 weeks, Jill reported that many of the issues she had sought counseling for had been resolved. These 5:1 positive interactions were actually preventing the bad behavior that she had seen previously. Her son, who was once defiant, resisted every request and every chore and picked a fight almost every time she opened her mouth, had become chill and seemingly happy. He might not have become mommy's best helper overnight, but she was seeing incredible improvement in how disrespectful he had been. In fact, he started reciprocating the positive interactions. He was saying "thank you" more often for simple things, like when his mom made dinner. He was more readily willing to show his homework because he believed he would receive praise rather than nagging. Most remarkably, he started to open up about some of his insecurities. Jill reported that this was especially meaningful to her because the very things she continually criticized him about were some of his greatest insecurities. Rather than feeding the fire of self-doubt through nagging, she created a place for her son. She could be a teammate and a support to him. She was now someone who could listen and encourage him when he felt low rather than belittle and discourage him. They still have their hard times. This principle won't change a person's fundamental personality, but it does work wonders when someone feels loved and appreciated. Unprecedented benefits come to teenagers when their interactions with the people they love are overwhelmingly positive.

When counselors mention this method to some parents, they are resistant and worry that they will simply be placating their child. They feel that being overly kind isn't necessary; they feel like they are treating their child with more kindness than is genuine. They might argue that when they are with a boss or in the "real world" no one is going to treat them that kindly or give them as many positive interactions. Although this guardian may be correct about it not being like the real world, home life shouldn't be the "real world." The real world is all around them. They will get negative treatment at school, in their jobs, and everywhere else, so protect their home life. Let home be somewhere that is safe rather than a place where they are in the school of hard knocks.

Too many relationships are toxic because people aren't kind enough to each other. In marriage counseling, couples are often told to treat each other like they did when they were dating. They held their tongue when they were bothered, they looked for reasons to compliment, and they chose to see the best in each other. After they say "I do" it can all change. There are couples who treat people on the street kinder than they treat their spouse. They save all of their patience for people around them that don't really matter in the long-run but treat those most important to them the worst. This happens all too often in families, and it most definitely happens between parents and children. Children treat their parents poorly; and, unfortunately, parents do the same. Kindness is lost in the home. So much so, that in many cases children may know that their parents *love* them, but do not believe that their parents *like* them. They don't feel that their parents enjoy being around them and the relationship suffers because of it. You want your child to know they are both loved and liked. Mom and dad offer kind words, give compliments, find the good, and go out of their way to show love. Many times parents don't even realize how negative their interactions have become. If you fear that this has happened to your relationship with your family members, especially your teenage child, resolve now to make the necessary changes.

In 1978, researcher Dr. Robert Nerem discovered something amazing about the power of kindness[6]. Dr. Nerem was conducting a study on heart health. They took test rabbits and fed them all the same diet and put them on the same exercise routine. Their goal was to see how certain lifestyles affect heart health. As expected, when rabbits ate a diet higher in fat and with little exercise, they developed symptoms of heart disease. All of the rabbits but one group developed severe symptoms. There was one group that, for some reason, was healthier than all the others. After searching for the reason why these rabbits were outliers, it was discovered that the only difference for these

---

[6] Harding, K. (2019). *The Rabbit Effect: Live Longer, Happier and Healthier With The Groundbreaking Science of Kindness*. New York: Atria Books.

rabbits was their research assistant. The assistant was a naturally kind, nurturing, and loving person. She would pick up the rabbits each time she fed them. She would talk to them, pet them, and give them love and attention. Amazingly, the rabbits who were part of her group were healthier than any of the other rabbits, in spite of their poor diet and lack of exercise. This groundbreaking and accidental discovery about the benefits of kindness helped to propel a whole division of research on how important kindness is to the development of all living things. If this kind of treatment is effective for rabbits, imagine what kindness can do for your growing child. It is not enough to feed, clothe, and drive them places. If caregivers want children to be their healthiest emotionally and physically, they have to show kindness.

Cultivating a Positive Inner Voice

As mentioned before, all of us have an inner voice. We talk ourselves through hard things, we figure out complex solutions, and, when we are bored, it is that same voice that runs through our mind. Think about your inner voice. You likely have had times in your life where your voice was negative, fault finding, and making you question your worth. Perhaps this voice creates anxiousness over whether people like you or whether you are loved. It is human nature to question your worth. The goal for caregivers is to help cultivate a positive inner voice for their children. The word cultivate is chosen intentionally. Just like we would nourish and care for a plant, we should nourish and care for our child's emotional and spiritual well-being. A loving guardian would never harm their child physically. Parents do a remarkably good job of making sure their kids have all the proper *things* to ensure their physical safety and well-being. Yet, the teenage years are a critical period for an individual to develop a positive inner voice. Many times their inner voice is *your* voice. The way you are talking to your child will show up at challenging times, either cheering them on or making them feel insecure. The kinder we can be in the small moments by increasing the positive interactions with our teenagers not only will strengthen the relationship, but will cultivate a positive inner voice that is nourishing with happy and supportive thoughts through challenging times.

Amazingly, many readers will find that increasing their positive interactions with their children might be the most influential thing they will learn from this book. Some parents find that this simple change is all they need to get transformative changes from their teenager. In my professional experience, this is the first thing that should be taught to any parent struggling with their teen. As guardians increase positive interactions, children may begin to open up, negative behaviors will begin to resolve, and their self-esteem will improve. Interestingly, I have found that many of us are so starved for positive reinforcement in our lives that when it is increased, we, both parents and teens, begin to feel hopeful about the future. We find realistic solutions to challenging problems and know we can do hard things. Don't underestimate the power of positivity.

CHAPTER 4

Setting and Creating Healthy Boundaries in The Home

So far the book has addressed a great deal about making teenagers feel loved, accepted, and that they have a safe place with their parents. As caregivers consider these virtues and how to implement them in their home, it may seem like more value is placed on "friendship" over setting clear boundaries. That is not the case. Children need strong boundaries, and they need to know the consequences if they can't abide by the rules of the home. However, boundaries and having a positive friendly relationship with your teen are not mutually exclusive. They can coexist; in fact, when they do, caregivers will see the best results.

Implementing Clear Boundaries

Whether you realize it or not, you have boundaries with every single person you encounter. There are social lines that are not okay to cross when you meet a stranger on the street. There are spoken and unspoken rules that dictate the relationship you have with your best friend. You know when you have crossed a line. To keep the peace of the relationship, you don't cross those lines. The problem arises when one person has an issue with the behavior of another but doesn't address it. Consider a married couple where one spouse is sarcastic and the other very sensitive to sarcasm. Over time, if the sensitive partner doesn't speak up about sarcasm hurting their self-esteem, the relationship and their self-esteem will become damaged. It is better to set those boundaries early on, as soon as an issue arises, so the relationship can be as healthy as possible.

As children enter the teenage years, parents will need to clearly communicate healthy boundaries often. Not only do guardians have to navigate learning their teen's personality, but to set clear rules about household behavior, morality, school, finances, and so much more. It is the caregiver's job to make sure that their youth have a fence in place so that they can safely learn about the world around them. If parents allow them to run wild without warning them of danger and negative consequences, the child will cross a line that doesn't just violate family rules; they may potentially break laws, be suspended from school, be dismissed from a job, and so forth. For this reason, caregivers should lovingly set boundaries for their teenage children. The rules and the consequences of breaking those rules must be clear to both the parents and the child.

How to Set Healthy Boundaries

In order to set healthy boundaries, caregivers should be discussing them and putting the rules in place *before* the opportunity to violate that boundary arises. If parents wait until after their youth has crossed a line, it can be more sensitive addressing it and getting them back on the right side of things. For example, if you talk to your child about curfew before they leave, you will likely receive a better response than if you text them at 11:00 p.m. telling them to "come home now!" They haven't prepared themselves to be home by 11:00. You might get more resistance than if you made it known beforehand. Ideally, the majority of family rules should be set before they even become an issue. Try to think about the things that were challenging or dangerous to you when you were a teenager. What kinds of boundaries or fences do you wish were in place that could have protected you from harm? What kind of boundaries did your parents place that you can see the value of and would like to implement in your own home?

Bradley Foster gave wise counsel as he explained that parents should intentionally parent their children by talking with their kids *before* they encounter something hard[7]. He relayed an experience of a father who sat with his 9-year-old child and said to him, "I was nine once too. Here are some things you may come across. You'll see people cheating in school, you might be around people who [use filthy language]. Now, when these things happen—or anything else that troubles you—I want you to come and talk to me, and I'll help you get through them. And then I'll tell you what comes next." He did this with his child at each age, from when he was 9 until he had a family of

---

[7] Foster, B.D. 2015, *It's Never Too Early and It's Never Too Late*, The Church Of Jesus Christ Of Latter-day Saints, Accessed August 2022.
<https://www.churchofjesuschrist.org/study/general-conference/>

his own. He knew that if he could get to his child before the hard stuff started, he could make the boundaries clear. This would help his son avoid getting into situations that might have compromised future opportunities for him.

Additionally, parents should have frequent discussions with their children about boundaries. This will enable the youth to feel as though they have a say in the decisions and the consequences that will be enacted if violated.

Here are some subjects that should be discussed early on:

Friends

Dating, relationships, and sex

Family chores

Curfew

Language (swearing and inappropriate language)

Bullying (both as victim and perpetrator)

Entertainment (movies and music)

Phone, internet, and social Media

Finances

Homework and schoolwork

Family relationships

Respecting people in authority (teachers, adults, law enforcement, etc.)

At the end of this chapter is a list of discussion questions or conversation starters to have with your child. Ideally, have these discussions *before* they become an issue. For example, you might as a family have certain rules about dating, and you expect your child to wait till around 14 to start exploring the idea of having a boyfriend or girlfriend. It will be most effective if you can have this conversation with them before they start a relationship, even as early as 10 or 11. It is harder to backtrack and change the rules when the child is 16 and already immersed in the world of dating. If clear boundaries are set prior to engaging in the behavior, it is easier on both parent and child. Many of these subjects will need to be addressed multiple times. Your 13-year-old will probably have a different curfew than your 17-year-old. There are big changes like getting a driver's license, working a job outside the home, or getting a phone that will change the rules. Try to reopen these conversations often so it is clear to the child what the rule is. Note: when you talk to your child about boundaries, let them feel like it is a discussion. This can be done by listening to them, validating what they say even if you can't implement it, and changing the narrative to feel like a conversation rather than a lecture.

How To Decide on Consequences

After guardians have had a discussion with their children and everyone has had their say, the rules should be clearly stated, and the consequence should be decided upon. The youth will do better with the repercussions if they know ahead of time what could happen to them if they break the rule. It is not enough to say, "be home by midnight," instead, it should be "be home by midnight, otherwise, you will lose friends tomorrow." Knowing ahead of time will do wonders in helping a teenager follow the rule. One of my children is a very black-and-white thinker. If we surprise him with a rule that he didn't know about, he will have a severe emotional reaction. He will fight it tooth and nail, because it isn't "fair." He argues that he can't be punished for something he didn't know was against the rules. I found that, with him, I couldn't predict everything that could go wrong; so many times, something has to go wrong before we can talk about it. From there we can set a rule and a consequence.

The question for many parents is how to set a consequence for their child. There are two ways to go about it. Parents can choose to do just one or the other, or they can do a mixture of the two.

The first is to choose something that works for this particular child and then use it as the blanket consequence for everything they do. For example, if your son loves video games and this is his preferred way of being entertained, losing video games could be at risk for any bad behavior. If this boy fails to do his homework, it could result in a loss of 30 minutes of video games that day. Ideally, in that 30 minutes, he does his homework. Some parents use this method by making the desired activity feel like a privilege and not a right. Consequently, they earn all of their video game time with good behavior. They can earn up to a certain amount a day if they do everything they should. Others choose to make video game time the standard. The child can play as much as desired unless they break the rules, then the video games are taken away. Note: Chapter 10 addresses finding the proper balance for healthy screen use and video games; but, for the purposes in this chapter, I will discuss using them as a reward or taking them away as a punishment.

If guardians choose to have a one size fits all approach to consequences using something that the teen loves, it will need to be something they actually value. Some parents choose to remove dessert or treats, time with friends, phone use, or even have the children pay the parents a fine when they break a rule. Any of these will work, as well as a variety of other consequences that aren't mentioned. The important thing is to choose something that the child actually values. If your child already doesn't love spending time with friends, then taking away friends won't incentivize them enough to want to follow the rules.

The second way to enact consequences is by choosing the most natural consequence for the action. This will look different for each family, but there are some similarities. For example:

Mean to family members- no friends for the day with the understanding that they will work on familial relationships.

Violated a family rule of going to a website that wasn't approved- loss of the internet or their phone for a week.

Broken curfew- next time they go out they have a curfew of 2 hours earlier or loss of car so parents come and pick them up at a desired time until they can earn back trust.

Didn't complete schoolwork on time - forced to work with a tutor or stay after school, losing time with friends to complete the work.

These are just a few examples of how caregivers can enact an opposite or logical consequence for rule breaking. Usually with this method parents take the opposite behavior, i.e., 'mean to family, so they have to spend MORE time with family. This acts as a way to help the child see how the consequences will be in the real world. Once they are out of the family home, they won't have someone helping them. Parents can show them now what natural consequences look like. In adulthood, the consequences come not from parents, but from bosses, low bank accounts, college professors, law enforcement, etc. Trying to enact the opposite consequence in the home from an early age can be a natural way to teach this.

In my experience, many parents use a mixture of the two. Generally, the use of logical and opposite consequences can be more effective, but it takes more creativity and time from the parent. In those cases, it is nice to be able to fall back on a general consequence. Having something in your back pocket that you know they love and value will help you to have an immediate punishment when you don't have a natural consequence in mind.

Follow Through

One of the hardest things about this whole idea of rules and consequences is the follow through. It requires parents to do just that. It takes a serious amount of intentional parenting and energy to enforce the rules. It requires observant parents watching the child for signs that rules are being broken and then preparing themselves for the discomfort that will come when they have to be the "bad guy" and enforce the punishment. This can be uncomfortable for many parents. It is important to remember why we have rules in the first place:

protection. It is a protection for the child and it is also a protection for the people that they interact with. When caregivers have this mindset, they can follow through with love and compassion, even though they will be the ones enforcing the rules and imposing the punishments. Consider this example:

Katelyn was 15 years old and an overall exceptional girl. She craved her parents' approval and was a decent student in school. At a church class, she received a conversation card where the teacher encouraged the youth to take the card home and have conversations with their parents. Most of the questions related specifically to safe internet, social media, and phone use, as well as proper conduct within their dating relationships. Surprisingly, it was Katelyn who pushed her mother, Mary, to have the conversation. Mary was surprised that Katelyn was persistent in asking when they could sit down without the distraction of household chores or caring for other siblings and just have this conversation. Mary knew she needed to take this opportunity, although, truth be told, she wasn't really in the right mindset or mood; but she set aside her other responsibilities and focused on the conversation card and Katelyn. As they conversed it was helpful to see where both Katelyn and Mary stood on certain issues, like the appropriate time to start a physical relationship with a boyfriend. Through talking about it in a loving and kind way, they were able to agree on some boundaries they would set in their home surrounding these issues. Mary had the understanding that it wasn't enough to just set boundaries; she needed to make it clear what the consequences would be if the rules weren't followed. This conversation happened over a year ago, but it has acted as the foundation for many more conversations that followed and has helped to soften the blow for Katelyn when she breaks a rule.

These conversations don't have to be made into a big deal. Sure, it would be fun if you took your child out to lunch and had a discussion with them over their favorite meal, but it isn't the only way to do it. Sometimes it is enough to just do it while you are driving to an activity, sitting on the couch after a busy day, sitting in the kitchen while you are making dinner, or while working in the garage. I have found that if the conversation is awkward for either parent or child (or both), you should keep the body moving while talking. This can be through walking, cleaning together, playing a leisure sport, or doing something to distract the body. It will feel more natural if it is a conversation on the side of another activity and not sitting on the couch looking each other in the eye and having a serious conversation.

Conversation Starters:

Phone & Technology

- When can I play video games, or games on my tablet/phone? Are there time limits to how much I can play?

- Are there certain games or types of games that are not allowed?

- What are the appropriate ways to communicate with friends/boyfriend/girlfriend over text? What ways are inappropriate?

- Can I send pictures to friends/boyfriends/girlfriends over text or message? If so, what type of pictures are ok?

- Who can I message over social media and who can't I?

- Will parents be checking private messaging?

- What sites am I not approved to visit?

- What should I do if I encounter pornography, dangerous content, or something that makes me uncomfortable?

- What are the rules with my phone and what are the consequences if I break those rules?

Dating & Physical Intimacy

- At what age do you think it is okay for me to have a "boyfriend/girlfriend?"

- When I start dating should it be in group settings or one-on-one dates? When is it okay to start pairing off?

- What is a good age to start holding hands, kissing, or cuddling?

- Do we have rules about sex? What should I know about practicing safe sex?

- Do you want me to tell you when I start a physical relationship with someone?

- What is coercion, rape, and sexual assault? Who should I talk to if I have been harmed?

- Is my significant other allowed in my bedroom? Am I allowed alone in a bedroom with someone else?

- If I ever feel my safety is compromised, how can I get out of that situation?

- What consequences should I be aware of if I break these rules?

Supervision

- What are the rules about being unsupervised with my friends/boyfriend/girlfriend?

- Do I have a curfew?

- How much should I tell you about where I am going and what I am doing?

- What punishments or consequences should I be aware of if I break these rules?

Finances

- When can I get a job outside the home?
- What expenses am I required to pay and what will you pay for?
- Do I have a budget? Can we make one together?
- Will you be giving me an allowance?

Family Responsibilities & Relationships

- What are my chores and responsibilities around the house?
- Is there a certain day or time of day that I need to have those chores completed by?
- If I don't complete these chores, is there a loss of privileges?
- What are the rules around sibling fighting, arguing, etc.?

Bullying & Self-Harm

- How do you define bullying?
- Who should I talk to if I feel I am being mistreated?
- How should I talk to a bully?
- How do I know if I am bullying someone else?
- What are the consequences if I mistreat or bully someone?
- What should I do if I want to hurt myself?
- Who can I talk to if I have feelings of depression, low self-esteem, or self-loathing?

Schoolwork & After School Activities

- What is the expectation for grades and schoolwork in our family?

- Who should I talk to if I am falling behind?

- Will you be talking to my teachers to keep me on track?

- What are the consequences if I don't complete my homework and schoolwork?

- Am I allowed to do after school activities such as sports, clubs, dance groups, bands etc.?

- Who is paying for the after-school activities? Am I required to pay for any of it?

These are just some ideas for conversation starters to have with your kids. This is not an exhaustive list. You may find that your child needs more conversation about some topics and less on others. Additionally, you might find that you need to discuss more topics than what are outlined in this chapter. As you start discussing these topics more openly, you will find that the conversation evolves naturally to become a discussion that reflects the specific needs of your child. Some kids may need very little discussion on schoolwork because they naturally push themselves at school, but they may need some extra guidance in healthy use of social media. The goal is to have these conversations with your teenager prior to them becoming an issue. It is so much easier to reference an earlier conversation you had where the rules were clearly outlined and both the parent and the child agreed to the terms than it is to throw a rule at them while they are in the middle of something. They will fight you and resent you more if you wait until it becomes a problem. If your child is older and you don't have the chance to talk preemptively about an issue, there is still time. Do your best to choose times that are not stressed, when there is no contention, and both of you are calm enough to talk about sensitive topics.

CHAPTER 5

Developing Better Conversation Skills with Your Teen

As it has been explained thus far, conversation between parents and teenage children is vital. Many parents know this is important and might feel like all this information sounds great, but worry that their kid doesn't open up to them. It is true that some kids are more reserved than others. There are children that can't be quiet; there are others that it feels like pulling teeth to merely have them relay the events of the day. While children are young, caregivers should be encouraging open communication. If parents want their youth to talk about the big, important things they have to be willing to talk about the small, seemingly unimportant things. If guardians shut down every conversation children want to have with them about sports, Pokemon, music, friends, Barbies, and anything in between, they can pretty much guarantee that their children won't talk about things that are significant. Consider this example:

Ever since Gavin was little, he had an obsession with Minecraft. Neither of his parents were into video gaming. They were not only bored when Gavin talked about Minecraft, but also worried. They were troubled that their son was obsessed with video games and seemingly had no other interests. To try to encourage other interests, whenever he would bring up Minecraft, they would shut down the conversation. Since Gavin thought about Minecraft often, he didn't have a lot to say to his parents that wasn't related to Minecraft. Over time his parents wondered why Gavin stopped wanting to talk to them about things that excited him.

Gavin's parents could remedy this situation in one of two ways: 1) If they didn't like the topic of conversation because it focuses too much on something they didn't value in their family, like video games, this doesn't mean all conversation has to stop. Instead, they could redirect the conversation to topics that are similar without going into territory they aren't comfortable with. For example, with Minecraft, if they didn't want to talk about the video game itself, they could ask questions about architecture, buildings, and natural resources. They could ask, "What is the hardest thing you've ever built? Do you think you could do it in real life? Why or why not?" This can get the child still engaging even though the parent is pulling them away from the topic they don't want to encourage. Guardians could also ask things like, "If you had Legos would you be able to build the same things, maybe build an entire city with the blocks and no instructions?" The child will likely appreciate the creative option to take something that they love and use it in other facets of their lives. First, start with the thing they love, and then help them morph it into something that can be enjoyed together. 2) Parents need to understand that learning to love the things their kids love is a way of showing them we care. Just because dad doesn't value Minecraft, doesn't mean he can't give them some time to talk about it. He might even suggest, "Let's talk about Minecraft for 15 minutes, then I want to hear other things about your day." When he says this, he is careful not to make it feel like a chore or a compromise. Instead, he could say excitedly, "I know you want to talk about Minecraft so let's talk about it for 15 minutes; I will set the timer, then I can't wait to hear about your day."

For many, it can be especially challenging when their child wants to discuss things that they can't get their head around. Maybe it's a type of music the parent doesn't know or like, their friends are annoying, or their interests are not the parent's interests. When it comes to teenagers, guardians should treat the many conversations about their interests like they would treat someone on a first date. They are kind and allow the other person to talk about themselves even though they might not really care. Their goal is to make their partner feel comfortable. As caregivers become more comfortable talking to their youth, they can start to be more authentic and tell them that they don't really love that music, topic, etc.

Many times parents feel like they are talking with their children about their interests, friends, or day to day, but can't get any deeper than the surface. For example, they might know that their teen is struggling with a friend group or in school, but all attempts to talk about it are fruitless. Luckily, there are some things that you can do to encourage more productive conversations with your child. Here are some suggestions:

Normalize It

Many teenagers feel like they are the only person to feel the way they do. Furthermore, they don't know how to put into words what they are feeling. For example, Evelyn was in 8th grade and had a lot of friends at school, but she had yet to find a *best* friend. Her mother, Cassie, perceived that Evelyn was feeling frustrated. She observed that Evelyn thought something was wrong with her. When Cassie tried to get her to talk about it, Evelyn would clam up. Rather than keep prying, Cassie said while driving in the car one day, "I was talking to my friend, Jessica and she said her daughter feels like she can't find a best friend. I remember not having someone who I really felt close to until college." Evelyn responded with, "Yeah right, everyone has a best friend." Her mom went further by adding, "No, I am serious. In movies it always seems like the person has this best friend who is always there for them, the two seem to be inseparable, but that isn't realistic. Have you ever felt like you have lots of friends, but still no one you are really close with?" The goal here is to help Evelyn feel like she isn't alone. Normalizing her problem helps Evelyn see that it is a problem that everyone deals with.

Usually, a parent will perceive a problem before the child will actually talk about it. The parent might worry about things like fitting in, drugs, bullying, problems in school, etc., but the child won't open up. Normalizing it by saying "{someone} is dealing with this problem, have you ever felt that way?" can be a softer way for them to open up and take away the fear that they are the only one with this problem.

Favorite Thing and Worst Thing

For some, the child is pretty good about talking, but isn't great about getting deeper. Everything is superficial. In this case, try focusing the conversation by saying to them, "Tell me your favorite thing that happened today and the worst thing that happened." This will help them to focus their thoughts on the things that are most important. This will also help you determine what is important *to them*. If a teenager is always saying that food was their favorite part of the day and a certain friend was their worst part, it can be an opportunity to dig a little deeper into both. It can empower parents to understand why their child enjoys dinner as a family as well as why they were upset with friends.

Name the Emotion for Them

Teenagers are awful at understanding their emotions. Because of their developing bodies, their moods are all over the place. It can be hard not only for the parent but for the child to know what they are feeling and why. It can be helpful for the parent to equip them with the right words to express themselves. For example, if your child is agitated, you might say to them, "It seems that you are feeling agitated or annoyed, is that right?" The important thing is to say it in a loving, non-threatening way; you are trying to help them, not scold them. Emotions are not the enemy. Emotions are natural for all of us. Humans cannot always control the way we *feel* about certain situations. We can, however, control the way we *act* when we feel those emotions. If a teenager is feeling agitated, they need to know that they cannot lash out at family members and younger siblings. They may *feel* agitated, but they can't *act* rudely. If a caregiver perceives that their teen is agitated, they could take them aside and say, "I see that you are annoyed, is that right?" If they agree, the parent can probe further with, "Did something happen today that is making you feel frustrated?" Sometimes the child won't know why they are frustrated. It takes a lot of emotional maturity for anyone to be able to determine why they feel the way they do. Don't expect a teenager to have this emotional maturity when they are just learning to regulate their emotions. Usually, the youth will say some sort of blanket statement like, "it was just a hard day." This is an opportunity for the parent to take the child aside in a loving way and talk about what is hard for them.

As mentioned earlier, many teenagers do not even know why they feel the way that they do. They might feel "stressed" without knowing why. Let's revisit Evelyn and Cassie. Evelyn is often upset and doesn't know why she feels upset. At the end of the day, she will be snappy and mean to her younger siblings. Cassie believes that she acts this way because of her insecurities or because something has happened during the day to make Evelyn doubt herself. When Cassie asks, "Why are you feeling so agitated?" Evelyn will yell, "I don't know! I just feel so annoyed, and they won't leave me alone!" Rather than yell back, Cassie takes this chance to have some one-on-one time with Evelyn. She can't leave the house because she has younger children, so once she gets the others settled doing something else, she and Evelyn will go to a quiet space, and they will dig together. Here is an example of their conversation:

Cassie: Did something happen today?

Evelyn: Not anything I can think of. It was kind of a normal day, but I just feel so uncomfortable.

Cassie: Okay, let's talk about why you might be feeling this way. Think about your interactions with your friends or kids at school, did you have anything that made you feel uncomfortable?

Evelyn: *gives a lot of different interactions, none of them red flags.*

Cassie: Wait, did you talk with Tia today?

Evelyn: No, I haven't seen Tia for a while. She is kind of ignoring me and Maddie. It's like all of a sudden she doesn't want to be with us. I haven't seen her for days. She eats lunch somewhere else and she doesn't really talk to me in class anymore.

Cassie: How does it make you feel when she ignores you?

Evelyn: Confused, I guess. It makes me wonder what I did wrong, or if she doesn't like me anymore.

Cassie: Do you worry about that a lot, that people don't like you?

Evelyn: Yeah, I mean, doesn't everybody?

Cassie: Yeah for sure, everyone does, even I do! But when you worry about people liking you, does it make you feel like you have to act like a certain person to get friends and people to like you? Do you put a lot of effort into getting people to like you?

At this point Evelyn starts to really open up into how tiring middle school is; how much time and energy she puts into keeping friends happy, talking to new people, and trying to fit in.

Cassie: It sounds to me like you are tired. Performing socially can be really exhausting.

Evelyn: Yeah, I guess that's true.

Now that Cassie has gotten to the core of some of Evelyn's stress, she can help her find positive ways to help her cope with it. They decide together that Evelyn can have some alone time to decompress. When she starts to feel agitated with her siblings, it is a sign that she has been around people too long and needs to take some time for herself. They decide that Evelyn can go to her room and read, take a bath or long shower, listen to music, or watch a short episode on TV by herself.

This might look like a therapy session, because in a way it is. A parent can become like a counselor to their child. They can help their child discover the root of the problem and teach them how to regulate their emotions. The goal for parents is to get them talking and let them express themselves *before* they start naming the emotion. Parents need to do three things for them:

1. Help them identify the emotion they are feeling.

2. Help them determine why they are feeling this way.

3. Equip them with healthy coping strategies to handle the emotion.

As parents have more conversations with their teens, they can start with these three tools. Eventually, both parent and teen will be less afraid of their emotions. The fear will be replaced with an action plan of what they will do. This will give them more confidence. This confidence comes from having an empathetic parent to whom they are strongly bonded to. As caregivers go through this process, the child is more likely to come to them, and even crave conversation with their parents when they feel upset.

Distract the Hands, Open the Mind

If the child is a hard nut to crack, try to distract their body so that their mind can open up. Guardians are probably doing this all the time without realizing it. If a parent wants to talk to their child but the child is feeling fidgety, agitated, or is simply ignoring others, get them to move their body. Go for a walk, play catch, ride bikes, etc. If a teen is resistant to physical exercise try playing board games, making a puzzle, or doing an art project- such as painting, crafting, sculpting, etc. This is a brilliant way for parents to help the child open up their mind. The goal is to get them distracted enough that they don't feel like the conversation is the main focus. Instead, they need to feel like the main focus is a sport or an activity and then the conversation is a byproduct. Think about the greatest conversations you have had with people–real breakthrough conversations. They usually came after some sort of shared interest, sport, craft, game, etc. Even eating can be a good distraction. Invite the child to go out for ice cream and, while sitting and eating, notice how much they open up.

Especially in the beginning, if caregivers do not have a good rhythm of conversation with their teen, it can feel awkward and unnatural. It can feel like it is forced. Don't give up! This doesn't mean having conversations isn't right, it simply means that it hasn't become comfortable yet. Coupling the conversation with some kind of other activity will really help both parent and teen to feel more comfortable.

Be There

If all else fails and there seems to be a barrier between parent and teen, just be there. Be physically present with the child as much as possible and eventually things will soften. Some children are not comfortable talking and need some time to build trust. Take advantage of every opportunity to be together. Here's how Meg implemented this with Darren.

Meg couldn't get Darren to talk, no matter what she did. Her other two children were open books and were constantly talking her ear off. In fact, it was exhausting always having kids talk to you. So the fact that Darren rarely wanted to talk or be around her was in some ways a relief. She cherished her time alone; she always said that Darren was the "easy" one. He took care of himself, did his own thing, and rarely gave her trouble. However, as Darren entered adolescence, she felt him pulling away. He rarely spent time with the family. When she asked him questions about his day, it was met with a grunt or one word answer. She honestly didn't know much about his life. She had to pry to get information about his friends, school, and his interests. It was almost like he was growing into a stranger she didn't recognize. Meg valued her time alone and usually loved doing things like grocery shopping, running errands, or attending other kids' activities and sporting events. She loved doing this alone because it allowed her time to read, listen to music, or just be with her thoughts; but she decided her relationship with Darren was more important. She started inviting Darren to go with her everywhere. Some of the time he flat out refused, but other times she would offer something he wanted to do such as, "I need to run and pick up an order from the mall; come with me and we will stop at the gaming store." If she offered something she knew he would want like a store, food, or activity; Darren would usually agree to come with her, although somewhat reluctantly. In the car, they wouldn't talk much, since Darren was reserved. She allowed him to pick the music, choose where they would go after the errand, and gave him as much control as she reasonably could. Meg reported that for the first month they literally just shared space. There was very little talking or even acknowledging that she was there. However, after a couple of weeks of spending so much time together, it got comfortable. It seemed like Darren even enjoyed their time together, even if he wasn't talking. Eventually, Darren began to see Meg as someone who would stick around, someone who really loved him, and, even more, someone he could trust. Even though Darren still isn't one to talk a lot about his emotions, he now opens up to Meg. In very natural ways, he tells her about his friends, what happens at school, and sometimes, even what he is feeling. Meg feels like Darren is still her easy kid because he doesn't require a lot of attention. However, because of that, it can be harder. She has to do a lot of work to make sure there is a strong connection between the two of them.

What you see from Meg and her feelings about Darren are very common for children who tend to be quieter, reserved, and self-sufficient. They appear to be easy, but if caregivers give in to that ease too much, they will miss out on the chance to create lasting relationships. This child might require more sacrifice to create a good bond, but it will be worth it in the end.

The Value of Good Conversation

This chapter may feel overwhelming to some. They might wonder if this much effort needs to be put into having healthy conversations between them and their child. For some parents and children, it does take a lot of work and energy, but it is worth the sacrifices. Guardians have only a few short years that their child is in their home, but even shorter in the critical stage of adolescence. For many individuals, this is the period of their lives where they choose who they want to be; they start on a path of maturing and deciding what direction their life will take. In psychology, there is a term called the "critical period." This defines a period of time when certain skills can only be learned during that time frame. Humans have many critical periods of development related to language, motor skills, brain development, and so forth. The adolescent years are a critical period of emotional development for an individual; parents simply cannot be bystanders and hope for the best. They cannot fall into the trap of believing that they can make up the difference when their children are adults. Yes, there are always second chances, but critical periods are essential to promoting learning and understanding these principles at an optimal age. It is worth the time and energy to develop a teen's emotional maturity so that they can learn to be confident and trust their caregiver as their mentor during complicated emotional periods. Parents will never know their child's hopes or the difficulties they are going through if they aren't actively communicating with them. This foundation will stem from hard work and a desire to communicate as often as possible. If guardians do this, they will see benefits not only in their relationship, but also in their teenager's emotional health. It is powerful for a developing youth to know that they have a parent who understands, validates, and loves them regardless of their weaknesses. This knowledge acts as a foundation for their self-esteem, self-confidence, and feelings of self-worth.

CHAPTER 6

Motivation and Your Teen

As a child reaches their teenage years, it is normal for them to lose motivation in activities they once loved. For example, school may have been a joyful and fulfilling endeavor for them during their elementary years; but, once they reach middle school, they seem disinterested, frustrated, and even burned out. This could be for a variety of reasons, but two of the most prevalent are a lack of self-esteem and increased workload paired with higher expectations as they enter a more competitive schooling environment[8].

Lack of Self-Esteem

Studies have shown that at least 50% of adolescents deal with what is considered clinically low self-esteem[9]. "Clinically" means that these teens are labeled as having serious distortions about how they view their body, personality, and/or general identity. Even though only half are said to have serious self-esteem issues, every individual can relate to bouts of self-doubt, low self-esteem, and feelings of low self-worth during their teenage years. Think about how younger children play; they go up to another similar aged child and just start playing or say something such as, "Want to be friends?" and bam! They've got a new friend! It's not as simple or easy as a teenager. Instead, they have to navigate more complex social situations. Making friends has become increasingly harder. These are likely some of the first times they have experienced rejection, not fitting in or just an overall feeling of being on the outside.

It is also important to note that a teenage child's hormones are unbalanced and constantly changing. Many of the feelings that they have about themselves might look and seem irrational to you. That is because they are. It has been shown that low levels of estrogen, which is a critical hormone in a girl's development, can be linked to irregular

---

[8] U.S. Department of Education 2003, *Department of Education Website*, United States Government, Accessed August 2022, <https://www2.ed.gov/>.

[9] ACT For Youth Center For Community Action 2022, *ACT For Youth Website*, United States, Accessed August 2022, <www.actforyou.net>.

levels of serotonin[10]. Imbalances of serotonin in the brain can contribute to depression, irritability, anxiety, moodiness, and trouble concentrating. Guardians might notice that their once sweet and easygoing pre-teen is now an unpredictable emotional monster. It may fluctuate from day to day, even minute to minute, where they stand with their moods. Parents shouldn't be overly concerned with these fluctuations; these are a normal byproduct of puberty. Instead, parents can take this period of heightened emotion as a chance to get to learn how their child likes to be talked to, comforted, or supported while they are feeling low, angry, or anxious. If caregivers allow it, this time can be a great time to learn how to manage their teenager's emotional well-being. This is an opportunity where every feeling is on the surface, so it can be easy to tell what emotion they are processing. Take advantage of this unique phase of life and try practicing some different ways of helping them while their emotions are raw and in the open. Eventually, their emotions will stabilize and it won't be a war zone. If parents can intentionally use this time wisely, the youth will begin to see their caregiver as an emotional confidant and mentor.

Academic Pressures

When considering self-esteem and school performance, there can be two possible explanations for a decline in motivation and performance. The first is that they now focus on social concerns over academics. It is very normal during this time of life to put more emphasis on friends and fitting in than on their schoolwork. This comes from lack of perspective and a desire to feel like they belong somewhere. Guardians may find that their child who used to obsess over impressing the teacher is now obsessed with impressing their peers. A teen may give in easily to peer pressure that school or homework isn't "cool" and stop trying. To combat the obsession with friends at the cost of their education, try introducing rewards that can help them recognize the value of school. Later in this chapter, ideas

---

[10] Pollie 2020, *Pollie Website*, Accessed August 2022, </www.pollie.co/blog/hormones-and-mental-health>.

will be presented on how to implement a reward system that will keep them motivated and help them regain perspective.

Most parents assume that their child's decline in school performance is because of the reason above; they are spending more time focusing on friends. Although this may contribute, it is likely not the only culprit for their decline. The second reason, which is less known, but very common, is the fear of failure. Many people, not just teenagers, adopt black and white thinking when it comes to their education. They fear failure. Rather than set themselves up for potential failure, they might choose not to try at all. This may look like they are disinterested in school, saying things like, "I don't care" or "It doesn't matter" when really what they are thinking is, "I am so scared I am going to fail that I would rather not try." At this point in their lives, there are so many aspects that are seemingly fragile, they may not feel like they can fail at one more thing. School and even extracurricular activities that they once loved might seem like too much of a risk. Accordingly, they stop trying altogether.

Elementary school is a special time for many children because many primary schools focus on the joy of learning. They have games incorporated into the learning, easier benchmarks to meet, and constant reinforcement to keep the child motivated and entertained. Often around middle school, the educational experience has transitioned from a positive learning environment to a more competitive one. This can feel overwhelming. Historically, school hasn't always been so competitive. In the past, teenagers were given more time and space to create, try new things, and even fail as they took time to decide what they wanted their academic future to look like. Now, many adolescents feel pressured to choose what they want to do with their professions as early as middle school. Kids are taking career placement tests as young as 12 years old to try to get an idea of what field they might be interested in pursuing. Although discovering likes and dislikes can be helpful in understanding oneself, parents and educators need to be careful not to push the child too hard. They should never facilitate the belief that their lack of academic success at this young age will determine their future success in the workplace. The stress on performance and grades can compromise the love that the child once had for learning. Instead, this environment can make them focus too much on their grades. They may be comparing themselves to other students rather than focusing on gaining knowledge.

Some of the fault for this can be placed on the educators who put undue pressure on the students through too much homework, competitive classroom environments, and not enough positive reinforcement; but some blame can also be put on the parents and home environments. By focusing too much on grades and performance, rather than learning, the parents are unknowingly causing more stress in their children.

Possible Solutions to Motivation Issues

One of the most helpful practices parents can implement is to focus on learning and becoming, rather than on performance. Scott Kaufmann has explored this very lack of motivation in youth and has stressed the importance of parents and educators adopting learning goals over performance goals[11].

Learning Goals vs Performance Goals

Learning goals are when benchmarks are met by simply learning or implementing something. If someone is learning to play a violin piece, they should set the objective for the day simply to learn a couple of measures well. Perhaps instead of saying, "I want to play this piece as well as the recording," they would say, "I am going to focus on a richer vibrato of the wrist, on getting my shifting quicker." These kinds of goals are focused on the fundamental skills of playing the violin. They use the piece as a means to improve or to learn certain techniques for violin playing rather than as a way to compare themselves to an imaginary standard.

---

[11] Kaufman, S.B. (2013) *Ungifted: Intelligence Redefined*. Philadelphia, PA: Basic Books.

If goals are performance-based, the violinist has taken the focus away from what they will become, as a result of their practice, to what they will achieve. Instead of having the objective be fuller vibrato, they might say, "I want to win the state competition with this piece." Or perhaps, they want to play it as well or better than the violinist on the recording. The problem with this type of performance-based goal is that no one can control all the variables and it sets the individual up for failure.

Let's look at a couple of examples of how performance vs. learning-based goals would look.

Example 1:

A teenager has signed up for the speech and debate team and has chosen to do an oratory speech for the competition. They write their own speech and memorize it. They practice with their coaches and are ready for the big day.

Focus on performance goals

If the focus is on performance goals, the child might say, "I want to place in the top three," or "I just have to be better than the person next to me," or "I need to qualify for the regional/state/national competition. If I can't meet these standards, I will consider myself a failure," etc. The parent might even perpetuate these thoughts by asking what place they got after the competition, or how they compared with the other competitors.

Focus on learning goals

If the focus is on learning goals, the child will say "I just want to be able to do the whole speech without messing up the memorization," "I am going to focus on putting more emotion into my speech," or "I am excited to share my hard work with the judges, because I know what it took to get to this point." One of the benefits of focusing on learning goals is that the individual sees how much they improved or learned while doing something hard. They feel successful in reaching their goals *regardless* of the outcome. In fact, winning or losing doesn't change the experience much for them at this point because their goal was based on learning and becoming. I guarantee that a teenager who has a fear of public speaking, but who chooses to push themselves by entering a speech and debate competition, will become more skilled and articulate regardless of any awards earned. A parent's goal is to reinforce that this, the learning and becoming, is *why* the child signed up for debate in the first place. Caregivers have to make sure that the child knows that even if *their* goal wasn't to just learn something, their parent's goal was just that: to see growth!

Example 2:

An individual is struggling in math. They might react in one of two ways: either feeling overly stressed or seemingly completely unmotivated to do any math. Most individuals, especially teens and pre-teens, respond to stress in one of these two ways. They could become increasingly stressed, agitated, and/or panicked. Or they might shut down, appearing to have lost all interest in school and math altogether. They could adopt a "what's the point" attitude. Regardless of the way, they respond to the struggle, focusing on learning goals will be beneficial.

Focus on performance goals

Setting performance goals for a school subject usually means focusing on the grade or test score. For example, a well-meaning parent might tell their child that they will give them a certain amount of money or reward for scoring well on the test. Usually, the reason the youth isn't performing well on the test is not because they are not motivated to get good grades. No one likes to look at a failing score. All children feel a stab of shame when they fail at something, even if they seemingly "don't care." Reinforcing that the grade is the determination of success can put more strain on the child to try to perform rather than learn.

Focus on learning goals

As the parent sits down with the child to see where the problem is with math, they should choose one or two *realistic* goals. The objective is to identify what they can do to improve their understanding of math. For example, if they are struggling with times tables and that is causing them to get the wrong answer when doing algebra, guardians could say "all I care about for this test/assignment/term is that we master those times tables." Then parents should consider ways to help their child better learn this skill. It could be using an app game that drills the times tables, asking questions in the car while driving, or even just doing them together in the evenings. When the child starts to master the times tables, this is when the caregiver gives the child the praise that they so immensely crave. Beware not to focus too much on the grade they are getting in math. Parents should recognize and help their child acknowledge that they may not "win" in math that semester and it is okay. It is more important that they *learn*, not that they get a good grade.

Many times teens, and even parents, forget what school, extracurricular activities, and childhood in general is about; it is about learning, NOT PERFORMING. Our high-stress, performance focused society would have us believe differently. To illustrate this principle, consider Raya. Raya did really well in elementary school, but was worried she wasn't fully prepared for middle school. Since she was such an exceptional student, her parents enrolled her in a more structured and competitive school for gifted students. As she prepared to enter the 7th grade, she got her class schedule. Within that schedule was a list of books that they would be reading and discussing in class. This helped parents and students know what to expect during the school year. Raya, who was primarily focused on performance, got a hold of the list and began to furiously collect the books. She spent time researching them and pushed herself to read them *before* the school year started. Raya's mother initially saw this as a sign of her daughter's intelligence and motivation, praising her for being a go-getter. However, as Raya and her mother talked further, her mother saw some red flags; the first being that Raya wasn't viewing school as a place to learn, but instead as a place to perform. Raya's mother took this chance to explain to Raya that she wasn't going to school to win; she was going to learn. No one expected her to enter the 7th grade already knowing everything a 7th grader should know. Her teachers understood that when she went to school the first day, she wouldn't know all of the 7th grade math, she wouldn't already know the significance of "To Kill A Mockingbird," and that most introductions to physical sciences would be new. In fact, the teachers were excited to teach! When Raya was given permission to simply learn, rather than feel like she had to perform, she started to enjoy school again. She knew that as long as she came back each day a little more informed than she was before, it was enough.

This is not a magic formula for getting good grades and performing well. When individuals adopt learning goals over performance goals, they might see some decline in their grades for a time. However, experts have made it clear that true learning and growth cannot be measured by grades or by a test. Malcom Gladwell, in "David vs Goliath," explained that many of the most successful professionals, entrepreneurs, engineers, inventors, etc., did not necessarily perform well in school[12]. In fact, many of these individuals had significant learning disabilities, such as dyslexia, that contributed to poor school performance. Yet, they were highly successful because they were able to focus on learning. They recognized that learning was the goal, not performing. Parents can set their teenagers up for long-term success by helping them to recognize the value of true learning rather than performing for grades. If they really are learning, their grades will begin to reflect it over time. However, this process will take patience on the part of the parents, students, and teachers.

---

[12] Gladwell, M. (2013). *David and Goliath: Underdogs, misfits, and the art of battling giants.* Harlow, England: Penguin Books.

Katie Millar Wirig, M.A.

Love vs. Expectation

When interviewing professionals and truly talented people, the question is often asked, "What inspired you?" For many, the answer is the love of the activity. In fact, a great predictor of whether or not the person will continue pursuing an activity is if they are enjoying it. Enjoyment will lead to the pursuit of an activity even if the person does not have a gift or natural ability. Humans seek love. Our brains are wired for pleasure. In one study conducted Benjamin Bloom followed a group of professional piano players to see how they got their start[13]. Many people assumed that because this group was extremely talented that they must have shown some real promise while they were young. Researchers hypothesized these students likely started with a strict professional piano teacher who set them up with a strong technical foundation. What they found was the opposite. They discovered that the individuals who made the piano into their professional career didn't necessarily start with a professional teacher. Most of them started with seemingly under qualified teachers, such as a neighbor or a family friend who loved music and conveyed that love to the child. These students were met with support, encouragement, a feeling of belonging, and a love for the piano. This is what propelled them forward to a successful career in music.

Many times parents assume that the way to get a child to do something is to convince them that it will serve them well or that it is the "right" thing to do. This tactic may work for some children, but as the child ages and becomes a teenager, they will increasingly gravitate toward the things that make them happy or that they enjoy. This should come as no surprise then that a teenager may not excel in math and just stop doing it all together. They don't love it, and during adolescence, they are driven primarily by emotion. Luckily, there are some things parents can do to help their child succeed at things that need to be done, which they may not love.

---

[13] Bloom, B. (1985) *Developing Talents In Young People*. New York: Ballantine Books.

Show Them the Value

Consider Lori and Alondras experience:

Alondra had taken cello lessons for years and decided all of a sudden that she was done playing. She resisted practicing and preferred hanging out with friends or playing on her phone to putting any real time into practicing. She still did the orchestra and enjoyed the social part of the group, but at home, she avoided playing the instrument. Rather than nag and push Alondra to play the cello, her mother, Lori, took a different approach. She found ways to show Alondra the value of the cello. For starters, she bought tickets to a concert where a cellist plays contemporary songs alongside a rock band. When Alondra watched the concert, she was filled with a deep love for the music, was awed by the talent, and craved being able to play like the solo cellist. Additionally, Lori would turn on music in the background of their home that was delightful, calming, and peaceful cello music. The hope was that Alondra would feel positive feelings while listening to the music. Lori helped to create positive experiences around the cello. For example, Alondra's cousin celebrated an important birthday followed by a religious ceremony. At the ceremony, Lori encouraged Alondra to play the cello while people came to their seats. Alondra agreed and was surprised by how many people commented on her talent. Their comments encouraged her to keep going as they expressed their desire that they wished they would have learned and stuck with their own musical instrument.

Lori did a great job of finding creative ways to show Alondra the value of the cello. If Lori had simply chosen to nag Alondra and say things like, "you're going to regret quitting," Alondra would have quit the cello months ago. Yet, Alondra is going strong and has discovered the value for herself. This tactic of illustrating the value of something that is seemingly undesirable can be done with practically any school subject, extracurricular activity, sport, club, or musical activity, etc. Find ways to show teenagers the possibilities of whom they can become if they stick with an activity. Soon enough, they will be propelling themselves forward without a parent or teacher having to push so hard.

Show Them How Hard Work Will Lead to Their Success

Something like math may be a bit hard to show a teenager why they love it. Several people really don't enjoy math and that is completely justifiable. Having different interests, thoughts, and talents is what makes life beautiful. However, just because a teen is disinterested in a certain subject doesn't mean that they can just drop the class or quit doing it. The way the American school system is set up, even through college, is to require students to learn a variety of subjects. It is required that you pass all of the subjects before you can move on to a specialized field. Therefore, if a teenager knows they want to go into law or something of that sort, convincing them they love math may not be possible. So instead of focusing on math, focus on their other goals. Map out what it will take for them to become a lawyer, politician, or professional public speaker. Show them the schooling and education they need and make it feel attainable. Cheer them on the whole way and give them as much information as you can to make them feel empowered. As caregivers do this, they will have to explain that, in life, there are simply hoops that have to be jumped through to get to the other side. Even if they want to be an attorney, they will have to pass a math class. Help them change their focus from how much they hate math to how much they will love the outcome. Help them visualize the benefit of finishing their math class and then being able to do what they really want to do.

Focusing on what the child loves will help them succeed more than any forcing, negative consequences, grounding, or nagging ever will. In fact, with most teens, if parents use negative motivators such as these, they will likely find it backfires. The teen will only become more resistant. They will also avoid doing the thing their parents want, simply so they don't have to hear, "I told you so." By helping the teen see that it was their idea, that this was their goal, and that caregivers are simply cheerleaders on the side, the youth will become empowered and succeed. When guardians do this, it improves the relationship between the teen and the parent. It will also give them a more solid foundation when it becomes harder for them to reach their goals.

A final note: Be careful not to make their success a power struggle—parent vs. teen. Teenagers crave independence, they need to feel like a decision is their idea, and they loathe feeling controlled. If the parent is a competitive person and enjoys taking credit, this may be a challenge. They may have to make some serious changes to switch from the driver to the passenger. In fact, even if the parent was the driver of the success, they will need to avoid taking credit. Instead, be generous in giving the child credit. If caregivers choose to fight a battle with their teen about math, school, music lessons, sports, etc., the child might dig in their heels because they don't want to be wrong. Instead, become a partner in their success by finding creative ways to help them succeed, and then, when they do, give them all the credit, even though the parent deserves much of it. By receiving praise and recognition, the teen will feel a sense of pride and independence that will propel them over the next mountain they need to cross.

CHAPTER 7

Sick, Tired & Over-Scheduled

We live in a world that is becoming increasingly busy. Some children spend more time at school than a typical adult's work day. Between transportation, time spent at school, and homework, teens and children have far less time to enjoy quality relationships with those that are most important. Now add to the mix all the extra clubs, classes, sports, and other worthwhile ventures, and a child can get over scheduled really fast. In some cases, it isn't the child that is over scheduled. The teen might have a seemingly unlimited amount of play time whether it be video games, TV, hanging out with friends, etc., instead it is the parent that is so over scheduled and busy that they are not able to spend much needed time with their family. All of us fall into the trap of giving our time to ventures that don't have any real value in the long run. We commit to things we don't want to do, we agree to projects that aren't essential, and we fill our time with things that have little redeeming value. We might believe that when we over schedule ourselves, we are just giving up our time, but there is so much more lost when we become too busy to have quality, meaningful time with the people we love most.

It can be hard to know when a parent has over scheduled a child or themselves. Each person is so different. Some thrive on being busy and don't like to be still. Even when they get a chance to relax they usually fill it with something. But there are others who benefit from more time to decompress away from the noise and the pressure of the outside world. The key is knowing what our child needs and when they are feeling too overwhelmed. Kim John Payne, author and psychologist, coined the term "soul-fever" to describe the phenomenon of when someone becomes ill in their soul from being too busy[14]. Think about it, when a child gets sick and runs a fever the parent is forced to slow down. They call in sick to work, the child misses a day of school, and time is spent snuggling on the couch. The caregiver watches the sick child very closely to look for signs that they

---

[14] Payne, K.J. & Ross, L.M., (2009). *Simplicity Parenting*. New York: Ballantine Books.

are getting better or worse. Simply put, the child's health is closely monitored, and it becomes the parent's first priority. Fever has a great deal of power. If someone is running a fever, that fever controls the day, both for the person who is sick and the caregiver. A fever is the body's way of telling the person, *you are ill, you need to slow down and take care of yourself.* What Payne explained is that we all get times when our body and mind are yelling at us to slow down, giving us clues that we are going too hard, too fast. Because there is no thermometer to measure how sick our soul is, we ignore it. When we ignore the signs and symptoms of a soul-fever, or when our soul and mind are sick and overwhelmed, we cause more damage to the body, spirit, and mind. It is during these times that caregivers need to stop everything they are doing and keep a close eye on the person.

What a soul fever or mental fatigue will look like will vary from person to person, but here are some common manifestations. You should note that usually, they will manifest in extremes. Example: while your child may not be a clingy person, they might do the opposite and be rude, mean, or difficult to the family. Look for extremes in behavior one way or the other.

Agitation

Depression

Jumpiness

Retreating

Stressed

Crying more than usual

Avoidance

Lack of interest

Trouble making decisions

Fatigue

Paranoia

Looking for ways to escape

These are just a few manifestations of mental fatigue. The parent's goal is to know their child well enough to be able to decipher when there's a problem. Just like a physical illness, caregivers know when a child isn't acting like themselves. When they have a virus, we know how to look for signs such as: sleeping longer than usual, forehead feels hot, or complaints of aches and pains. Parents are very good at determining when their child is physically ill, but too often we overlook signs that our child is emotionally ill. Rather than give them the care that they need, we pressure them to push through it. Instead of slowing down our lives to attend to their emotional health, we might ignore it. Or even worse, we may get angrier at the child for their behavior, when their behavior is an indicator that they are needing *more,* not less, love.

Attending To Your Child's Emotional Health

It would be wonderful if we could normalize the need for caring for our children and our own emotional health. When our child is suffering from soul fever they may act out and feel as though their life is too overwhelming, become moody, stressed, or anxious. When this occurs, we can respond in one of two ways. Compare these two reactions:

1. You see their distress and you respond with something to the effect of, "Cowboy up, the real world doesn't stop because you had a bad day, it will get worse when you're older. You don't even know how good you have it!"

   Or

2. You see their distress and you respond with something to the effect of, "I see that you aren't feeling well today. Why don't I pick you up after school and the two of us will go out and spend some quality time together?" During this time, you talk about their life; things that are good, things that are hard. You watch a show together, enjoying each other's company and

maybe even give them a couple of extra hugs throughout the day.

Let's compare the possible responses from your child to each reaction. First, even though you told your child to "cowboy up," it is not likely that they will magically get a grip on their emotions. You likely will find that it does the exact opposite. You belittled their experience by telling them that it gets worse and that they have no idea how hard life can be. This is the funny thing about us as adults. We *learned and grew* into adults. At 14 you didn't know how hard life could be, and thank goodness! You were given small life experiences that were stressful and you learned how to manage these small things so that as bigger responsibilities were placed on your shoulders you were prepared to take them. Your child is *learning* and a parent shouldn't belittle the process as the child learns to handle stress. The important thing to recognize is that parents can push through their own emotional fevers, but that is because they learned how to do it. Additionally, most of us aren't that good at taking care of our own emotional health. In many cases, adults are the very worst examples of recognizing when we are at the end of our rope and need to take a step back. The worst outcome of this scenario is that your child will dig in their heels and will feel like you don't understand, or even worse, that you don't care. You want them to talk to you about the big things. You want to be the person they come to when they are approached by a friend about using illegal drugs, underage drinking, safe sex, bullying, major life decisions, and so much more. If you respond to their emotional needs with undue judgment or belittling, you will close that door to conversations in the future.

On the flip side, look at the second possible reaction. You recognized that your child was suffering emotionally. You might have even felt like their reaction was disproportionate to the trigger. But when you saw that they were feeling sick in their soul, you took it seriously. In fact, you made their emotional well-being your first priority and I guarantee your child will notice. The time that you spend together to heal their soul, just like snuggling with a fevered child on the couch, will create a bond between you. Your child will feel seen, heard, and loved. They will also be able to process their own emotions and recognize when they need to slow down and care for themselves. They will know that their guardians give them permission to invest not just in their physical health but their mental health as well. The best outcome is that you will become a trusted mentor and parent. These small moments will plant the seed of trust between you so that when those hard topics come up, you will have a foundation to draw on. With enough time and trust, they will come to you when they need help with the big stuff.

What Merits a Response?

When presenting the idea of slowing down their children's lives to encourage mental healing, some parents worry that it coddles the child. They worry that if they took every day off work and excused their child from school each time their child complained, no one would work, and their kid would be a middle school dropout. I am not suggesting that every bad day be treated as a soul fever. Everyone has good days and bad days. What I am presenting is that there will be a few occasions when caregivers will see that their child is worn down. They will notice that it will be different from other simply "bad days." It might happen after many bad days have occurred in a row. It could be halfway through the school year and things are hard with their friends. A guardian will be able to determine if it is just moodiness or if the teen is feeling severe emotional pain. If parents are not able to tell, then watch the child more closely. Look for signs that things might be worse than they are letting on. And if in doubt, care for the child and err on the side of compassion and empathy. I cannot think of a time when I regretted being empathic to the people that I love.

Ava's Story

Ava had always been a talented and fun-loving girl. Her parents felt grateful to have Ava in their home. She was kind to her siblings, a peacemaker, and a creative thinker. Her parents would frequently find her thinking up some kind of game on the trampoline to make everyone have a good time. She really was just the perfect mixture of kindness and the life of the party. As Ava entered her teenage years, she showed her natural talent for gymnastics. She had done gymnastics recreationally in the past, but as she got older, she wanted to do it more competitively. When she wasn't at gymnastics, she thought about gymnastics, talked about it, and would hardly hold still. She also loved her friends. Friends were a big part of her life. When she wasn't at gymnastics she was with her friends. She would make sure to be up on time to complete her school work, so that any free time she had not doing gymnastics could be spent with her friends. Ava's mom, Tina, started to notice that in the evenings after a full day of playing, flipping on the balance beam, and stellar school work, Ava would become emotional. Many times at the end of the day before bed Ava would simply cry. When Tina asked Ava why she was crying, Ava couldn't even tell her why, she would just cry. Initially, Tina brushed it off as normal hormones for a teenage girl, but when it persisted, Tina began to worry. Rather than taking drastic steps to pull Ava from gymnastics, which Ava loved, she started implementing firmer boundaries. She limited how much time Ava could spend with friends and how demanding the school classes she was able to take. Tina would watch the clock and once Ava had played with her friends for a decent amount of time, Ava would be called home. Initially, Ava resented it. She didn't know why her mom was trying to control her. But Tina lovingly explained that she wanted to see if the reason Ava had been crying was because she was too overwhelmed and was wearing herself down. When Ava would come home, Tina and Ava would sit down and watch a TV show together, Ava's choice. They would eat ice cream and Ava was encouraged to just share everything about her day, her thoughts, and whatever else she needed to process. With school, Tina encouraged Ava to take only a couple of demanding classes so that in the mornings she could have more time to sleep in and less time spent on homework. Within days, that difference was noticed by all. Ava's nightly crying started to decrease. Yes, she still had teenage girl mood swings, but when she cried, she could usually tell you *why* rather than just a general feeling of hopelessness and fatigue. Tina saw in her daughter the sign that she wasn't caring for her emotional health so she took action. Tina placed things in Ava's life that allowed her to have a meaningful relationship with her family, rather than too much time with friends. Tina is also working on protecting chores, family dinners, and quality family time into their daily routine, hopefully giving her more balance between play, work and rest.

It is the parent's goal to be on the lookout for signs that their children's mental health has been compromised. Knowing that mental health disorders plague not just adults, but children and teens as well, it is imperative that caregivers, teachers, and coaches work together to ensure that growing children are given the space they need to learn how to care for their mental health. If this is hard for you, remember that just as we all learned to walk step by step and fall down, your child is learning, step by step, how to manage their mental health. Don't expect them to have the emotional maturity of a well adjusted adult when even parents are terrible at caring for their mental health. Intentional parenting is required to determine if a child needs to heal from a "soul fever." If mental fatigue is present, use patience and compassion to assist them in getting the healing they need.

CHAPTER 8

Handling Emotional Outbursts with Intentional Parenting

As stated earlier, teenagers' lives go through a range of emotions for a myriad of reasons. Many times, when parents seek advice from professionals it is to help manage the emotional unpredictability of their teenager. A teenager usually shows their emotions in one of two ways: they bottle up the emotion and then explode after a long time has passed or they might feel the need to express every annoyance or frustration that comes to their mind, making them seem continually grouchy. The way each child expresses their emotion will depend on their personality and their individual style of communication. Understanding how your child communicates will be very important to your success in helping them navigate their negative emotions. Think back to when your child was a toddler and they would get hurt. Try to remember how they reacted. For some children, stubbing their toes and breaking their arm sounded like the same scream. Their reaction to a minor injury and a serious injury was the same. For others, they were pretty chill, so when they did cry over an injury the parent knew something was wrong. This same pattern has likely continued into adolescence. Knowing if they react emotionally to minor triggers will help determine if their emotional outbursts are serious, or if they simply are an emotional person who occasionally needs to blow off steam. Whether the outbursts are happening often or whether they are rare, parents can benefit greatly from knowing how to help their children manage their complicated emotions.

You Are Their Solid Object

Much of the teenage years are spent feeling out of control. As youth deal with new emotions, new situations, new friends, new schools, etc., they will likely feel as though everything is novel and therefore beyond their ability to control. Feeling like they can't control their environment, or their life is a major stressor for anyone. That is, *unless* they feel like someone close to them is in control. Imagine traveling to a new country. You don't know the language, the culture, or how to get around. Luckily, a friend of yours agrees to go with you because they are familiar with the country, they speak the language, won't get lost, and know all of the cultural norms. Now imagine that while in this new place, you experience a distressing situation, and in your panic you turn to your friend. Your friend is in complete control. This friend gives you the proper instruction on how to handle the situation; they also translate what was said so you can respond appropriately. Immediately, you feel comforted knowing that if your friend isn't panicking, neither should you. The situation is in control, even if it isn't you that is controlling it. This friend is solid for you and because of that you feel calmer even though you are navigating a new place.

This illustration is similar to an individual's feelings as they navigate transitioning from childhood to adulthood. They will often feel out of control. Small things that wouldn't bother a mature adult, will bother them, and their reactions might be disproportionate to the situation. The parent's goal is to be like this friend in a new country; they don't have to do everything for them, but they are there to help them feel calmer and safe if trouble arrives. This comes from showing them that their guardian is in control, that they are a solid, immovable object in their lives. Caregivers can be this safe person for their youth even during an emotional outburst.

People who are versed in other parenting methods might be familiar with the idea that they should aim to be unemotional during an argument or a fight. This is a commonly used tactic because it is effective. Fire can't be fought with more fire, so if a child is emotional and volatile a parent cannot calm the situation down by escalating it themselves. People become emotional when they feel strongly. For many teenagers, when they become emotional it escalates to a feeling of being out of control. They don't know how to handle their huge emotions and so these emotions become bigger and bigger while they become more and more concerned that these emotions are taking them over. A teenager may not understand this feeling rationally; at the moment, chances are that they aren't thinking at all, but regardless, they are feeling scared and out of control. This is the parents' chance to put on their game face. Here is what this "game face" includes:

1. Set your own emotional reactions aside. Do not be reactive. Instead, try to simply listen to your child. Determine what they are saying underneath the irrationality they are expressing. Keep your face steady. Don't let them rattle you. When you are calm you are telling them, you are safe, I have control of this, you can't unhinge me.

2. Don't engage with emotional biting responses. If they yell at you, "you never let me do anything!" Instead of saying, "Really, *you never* get to do *anything?* Do you have any idea how much I do for you? Everything in my life is for you, you, you!" You could try, "What would make you feel that way?" Allow them to discover their own irrational thoughts. Additionally, by letting them come to their own conclusions they will see the error in their logic. Asking them a question can help both of you since the answer may surprise you. When you ask this basic question about their feelings, you can get insight into why the individual is feeling the way they do.

3. Don't get defensive. They will attack you. It will feel personal. You will feel the need to defend yourself. Remember their outburst is about them, not you. They will try to make it sound like it is about you, but it is not. It is their reaction to feeling out of control. If you make it about you and the need to defend yourself, they won't feel like you are solid. If they become truly offensive or mean, you can stop the conversation and calmly say, "You have crossed a line. I will talk to you, but not if you say disrespectful things. Let's take 10 minutes and then revisit this." Set the timer, and if they won't leave, you can walk away and come back when the timer hits ten minutes. You can reopen the conversation and say, "So you felt like…." And then stop the conversation again if they become overtly rude.

4. Set your knee-jerk reactions aside and think through what you will say before you say it. View all reactions through the lens of "how will this affect them?" For example, if your child

comes to you to tell you that they did something wrong, stop yourself before you give a knee jerk reaction of, "How could you be so stupid?" This will only trigger a fight where they feel like they need to defend themselves. Instead, hold your game face, close your mouth before you let something come out that isn't well thought out, and instead try saying, "Why do you think you made that decision in the moment?" Hopefully, from there it will open a conversation about deeper things the child is dealing with. For instance, if the child cheated on a test and you ask, "Why did you feel like you needed to cheat?" It could open a conversation about low self-esteem, peer pressure, school pressure being too much, etc. This doesn't mean that you are excusing the cheating, it will be dealt with, but it helps you understand the child better, and how you can avoid it in the future. Usually, bad behavior is the symptom of something deeper. If you give a negative knee jerk reaction to a bad behavior, it will put them on the defensive and you will never get to the root and actually solve the problem. If this is hard for you, try counting to five or ten seconds before responding.

5. This message of "I am in control, you are safe, I am constant for you" can only come if it is true. You must be able to show your child that hard things can happen without losing all control over our emotions. This might mean that you have to work personally on yourself and how you process challenging things. If you are a highly reactive person and your emotional reactions are usually disproportionate to the trigger, start now by working on processing tough emotions without escalating.

If this feels hard to accomplish, you are right. This is something that you will spend a lifetime perfecting and may never arrive, but it is worth the effort. Consider this story.

James was the father of three children. His second oldest child, William, was easily the hardest of all the children. Since the day he was born he always had big emotions. He was either very happy or very angry, and unfortunately, it felt like the majority of the time, he was angry. As William grew older his parents hoped that he would mellow out, but this was not the case. As he reached his teenage years, he only seemed to become more irrational with his emotions. James and his wife, Becky, would try to tag team William because both of them became very overwhelmed while trying to manage their emotions. James especially was just fed up. He was tired of his home life being so volatile. He decided to seek out additional help. James was advised to try being a solid, unemotional object in the home and to implement this type of communication when Will became worked up. Initially, it seemed impossible. James was an emotional person himself and he felt like Will needed to be told that he couldn't be so aggressive and mean. He worried that by being unemotional it would be like giving in and letting Will win. However, he was tired and desperate enough to try something new for a couple of months. It didn't take long before the opportunity came to use his new skills. Will became upset about not wanting to go to a family party they were scheduled to go to. In the past, Will would start yelling, insulting, and digging in his heels. James would yell back, telling him to get in the car, and maybe even try to drag him (which was unsuccessful.) After both of them were tired from yelling and fighting, Will would go to hide in his room. As a result, James would be too angry to go, and Becky would take the other two kids to the family party and make up some excuse as to where James and Will were. This time though, James decided to try something different. Here is how it went:

James: Hey Will, heads up, we have a family party tonight. We will be leaving around 5:00.

Will: I don't want to go. I hate those people.

James: (show no emotion at the rude remark from Will) Why don't you want to go?

Will: Because I already said I hate those people! All they do is talk about things I hate. That's the last thing I want to do. I would rather stay here and do NOTHING; literally stare at a wall, than go see them.

James: I didn't realize you didn't enjoy yourself when we were there. Is there something we could do differently while we are there to make you feel more comfortable? (Still straight faced and unemotional)

Will: Yeah, never go there again. No wonder you want to go, you are just like them, boring and stupid. (Trying to get an emotional reaction out of his dad).

James: I do enjoy spending time with them. We still have an hour before it is time to go. If you can think of something we could do there that would make it more enjoyable, you can tell me and I will see if I can work it out.

Will: Yeah right, you don't care about me! (Trying to make his dad feel guilty, making him choose between Will or James' family)

James: (Feeling tired of the run around, but sticking to it) I am happy to try and make you feel more comfortable. I am open to suggestions.

Will: Fine... I would like to play football while we are there.

James: I am not sure if we will be able to get a full game going, but I can ask your grandmother if we can put a football game on the TV. That way if you aren't enjoying yourself, you at least have that. Would that work?

Will: Fine, I guess. It is better than having to talk to those idiots.

James: (Not reacting) We will leave at 5:00.

Even though this doesn't seem like a win because Will is still rude and his dad may look weak to you, James is actually the one in control and James "won". They both will be going to the family party and Will's rudeness didn't get the reaction he wanted. He didn't rattle his dad. Let's look at what it would usually look like:

James: Hey Will, heads up we have a family party tonight. We will be leaving around 5:00.

Will: I don't want to go. I hate those people.

James: You watch your mouth, young man. Those people have been good to you and you are acting disrespectful.

Will: I do hate them! All they do is talk about things I hate. That's the last thing I want to do. I would rather stay here and do NOTHING; literally stare at a wall, than go see them.

James: Oh really, you would stay here and stare at a wall? You have never sat still for 5 minutes. Why do you have to make everything so dramatic? You know we go to your grandmother's every Monday.

Will: Yeah, and I hate it every time. No wonder you want to go, you are just like them, boring and stupid.

James: How dare you talk to me like that! One more comment like that and I will make your life miserable. We are leaving at 5:00 and you will be in the car and you will be happy or you will wish you weren't alive.

Will: Yeah, I bet you wish I weren't alive! You don't care about me. Of course, you would choose them over your own son.

James: Of course, I would choose them. They don't make my life miserable. You do this EVERY TIME we try to do anything. You ruin it for me, your mom, and your other siblings. You are the most selfish person in the entire world.

Will: I'm selfish? How about you...

Then a full blow name calling fight breaks out ending with Will in his room and James so angry and feeling guilty about things he said that neither of them goes. As you can see from these two examples, in the first James keeps his cool, and most importantly, he is in control. He is willing to make Will feel comfortable but is unwavering in the fact that his son will go to the family party. In the second example, James is still unwavering in making his son go to the party, but he is not in control. Because of this, James is unable to convince his son. What an outsider may not realize about this interchange is that when James reacts emotionally to his son's taunting and disrespectful attitude, Will actually gains control of the situation. He knows what he can say to his dad to upset him and once James is upset and emotional, Will is more likely to get what he wants. It is more likely that his Dad will walk away, ignore his son, and be so angry that he will say, "do whatever you want, I don't care." Even though Will may not be consciously trying to make his dad miserable, he is stubborn and a fighter. He will do what it takes to get what he wants.

Not all teenagers fight this way. This is an example of a child who is strong-willed, values being right and is fiercely independent. All of these can be fantastic qualities if he is taught how to foster these skills in a way that brings out the good in others and the good in himself. Not every family may have a child like Will, but they may have a child who tries to get their parents to react emotionally, allowing them to get what they want. Here are some common ways a teenage child might do this.

Guilt

Examples include: "You don't love me," "I wish I were never born," or, "You like her more than you like me."

These kinds of statements are used to elicit guilt from the parent. When you are in the middle of a fight or when your child is trying to get something out of you, they may say something to try to make you feel guilty. A parent may even stop and wonder, "am I treating this child unfairly?" Seeing them in pain makes us feel pain and our instinct might be to prove to them, at that moment, that we love them. Instead of reacting to these types of statements by giving them what they want, stay unemotional until you get through the fight. After some time has passed, and the child is no longer emotional, a parent can explore these statements to determine if the child really does feel deprived. For instance, if a parent has a depressed child, a child who feels victimized, or if there is some underlying jealousy towards another sibling, they may benefit from additional love. Some questions caregivers might ask during a controlled and unemotional conversation are, "What can I do to make you feel more loved?" or, "Do you have some activities you would like to do together?" And then the parent can give more focus to giving them lots of love throughout the day *if* they are worried that this is a legitimate concern. However, know that in the middle of a fight, it is likely a tactic being used to make the parent feel guilty so that the teen can get what they want.

Insults

Examples include: "You're the worst parent ever!" "I hate you!" and name calling.

Another common tactic to use during a fight is name calling and insults. These come out of anger and we all do it at times. During moments when we feel that someone is standing in our way, we feel intense anger toward that situation and perhaps even that person. Parents should expect that at some point their child will say some of these things to them. This is a natural reaction to craving independence without being able to fully stand alone. They push back against the person or thing that is standing in their way. If a child is really clever, they might even attack a weakness that they know their caregiver has. For example, with Will, he knew how much his dad loved his family, so he would insult the family and his dad. This was hurtful to James because he not only loved his family, but his family had helped them so much, including Will. Even though Will was completely out of line to talk about his family that way, if James loses control over his emotions, he allows Will to take over. Instead of becoming emotional, parents should ignore the comment and stay straight-faced. This will show that insults aren't worth dignifying. And secondly, the guardian can stop the conversation. Try saying, "You crossed a line, and we will resume this in 10 minutes." As mentioned before, walk away, and let the child sit there for a while, hopefully causing them to calm down. Set a timer so that the child knows how long they have to think about the line they crossed. It is important that the child doesn't leave during this time to go listen to music, play with friends, or do any other activity. They need to just sit for those 10 minutes. Once the time is up, the conversation can resume and the parent can gently and without emotion let them know that they want to work out the problem, but there will be no name calling or insulting.

Whining

Examples include, "Please I want it so bad," "I promise if I get this; I will never ask for anything again." Or, "Please, please, please."

Whining and begging are normal part of life for any child. In fact, whining is the most commonly used tactic for younger children, especially toddlers. The goal is to wear down the person until they just give up and say yes. As a teenager, it may look different than when they were a toddler, but the goal is the same, to wear parents down until they give in. Once again, this is all about control. The underlying emotion the caregiver will feel is generally annoyance. The parent will become so annoyed with the child that eventually they will say, "Do whatever you want, just leave me alone!" If a child is prone to whining, guardians will want to stop it as soon as they can. First, the parent should let them know that they already gave the answer and that they won't be talking about it again. Second, if they continue to whine, the caregiver can start to remove additional privileges. For example, a child wants to go to a sleepover at a friend's house. The parents told them they could stay for a late night, but could not sleep over. Each time they ask again, they will lose 30 minutes off the time. Eventually, if they ask enough, they won't be able to go at all. It is important to make sure to let the child know *why* the answer is no. Back to the sleepover, the parent will need to make sure they tell them a reason, such as, "We do not allow sleepovers in our family, it is not a safe environment and sleepovers are where questionable things happen. It is non-negotiable for our family, but I am happy to take you for a late night." Once the parent has said this, they can either repeat this same statement, or say, "You already know the answer." Don't keep trying to explain it and give more reasons. They already know the reason, that is enough. If they continue, start removing privileges, or counting to three. Once you get to three, another privilege is taken away.

These are just a couple of ways that a child might get a parent to emotionally react to them. Remember that even though they seem to want us to give in, they are testing the boundaries and testing us. They want parents who are solid and steady, even if they don't think they do. As they navigate the transition from childhood to adulthood, they need to know that their parents are in control and are constant. We can still change our minds and negotiate with our children. There will be plenty of that. But when they have an emotional outburst, we are there to help them navigate it by showing them how to control their emotions, how to safely and calmly get what they want, and most importantly, that we are there to help them with love, logic, and control.

CHAPTER 9

Healthy Touch: Why Your Teenager Needs It and How to Make It Natural

Remember when you brought your new baby home and you couldn't get enough of their soft skin and snuggling? If you were like most parents, it was hard to put your baby down. Both of you wanted to be close at all times. Think about how much time out of the day you actually spent touching your child. You had to carry them everywhere because they couldn't walk yet. While they ate a bottle or nursed, they were held close to the chest. When you changed their clothing or diapers, you touched their skin, arms, and legs. Even when they slept, you often held them. Throughout the day your child was flooded with touch and love from their parents and the people around them.

Touch is a vital part of any person's development. In a study done in Romania, researchers looked at the long-term effects for children who hadn't been held or touched enough[15]. They compared children who had spent at least 8 months in an orphanage as infants to children who had lived in a loving home with parents who had physical contact often. They found that by age 6-12 the individuals who hadn't had physical contact suffered psychologically from the lack of touch. These children suffered greatly. In addition to some individuals developing actual physical illnesses, these children showed an overwhelmingly large amount of cortisol in their blood. Cortisol is the hormone that causes stress. These children who lacked physical touch developed an overactive stress response, much like a person who has experienced repeated trauma. This stress response follows them for the rest of their lives and will cause them to be on heightened alert, including having a harder time self-soothing.

Parents reading this book know it is likely that their child experienced plenty of physical affection in their infant and toddler years. It was probably very natural for caregivers to love their children

[15] Gunnar, M.R., Morison, J., Chisholm, K., & Schuder, M. 2001, *Salivary Cortisol Levels In Children Adopted From Romanian Orphanages,* Dev Psychopathol, vol 13, no.3, pp. 611-628.

through touch. But as these children develop into teenagers it can be harder to know how to appropriately show love through touch. Yet, teenage children need love through physical affection, perhaps as much as they did when they were infants.

Multiple studies have been done to look at the need for touch in people of all ages, from infants to the elderly. Their findings were conclusive that touch plays a vital role in not just infants' development, like the Romanian case outlined above, but also that adolescents and teenagers need touch just the same. Tiffany Field compared children and adolescents in both Paris and Miami looking at how much the children were touched[16]. The Paris parents touched their children more often through hand holding, hugging, patting, and sitting close enough to touch bodies than the Miami parents did. It was discovered that these children who had more touch showed a statistical significance of being less aggressive both physically and verbally. The study continued to observe families and couples in airports across the United States. It was determined that people were touching each other less and less. They found that children were entertained by devices, couples were distracted, and there was little touching. This was especially true for the parents in the United States compared to those in Paris. The Parisians seemed to be looking for opportunities to show love through touch. Additionally, because of the increased reporting of negative touching in abusive relationships whether in schools, homes, or communities, many caregivers and mentors are worried about what kind of touch is appropriate and what is not. Rather than toe the line, teachers do not touch their students, even to give an encouraging pat on the back, or a hug when the student needs extra attention.

---

[16] Jones, J & Field, T. 2018, *Greater Good Magazine,* The Greater Good Science Center At University of California, Berkeley, Accessed August 2022, < https://greatergood.berkeley.edu/article/item/why_physical_touch_matters_f or_your_well_being>

Katie Millar Wirig, M.A.

Oxytocin

There has been an overwhelming amount of research done about what happens when a child isn't touched enough. It is clear that cortisol and the stress response are activated. There has also been a great amount of research conducted to conclude that positive touch is critical, even for an individual that has lived a happy, healthy life as an infant. Over the years there has been an abundance of information that has been gathered about the role of oxytocin and the positive effects it has in humans. Oxytocin is sometimes nicknamed as the nurturing or comforting hormone. When a person has oxytocin in their body it makes them feel safe, comfortable, and loved. It is essentially the opposite of cortisol. Four researchers conducted a comprehensive study to determine the effects of loving touch and how it affects the human brain[17]. It was concluded that when people are touched by friends, family, and even acquaintances, it releases oxytocin, thereby creating bonds of trust, friendship, less stress, and an overall feeling of well-being.

As children get older it may feel uncomfortable to touch them because you are not sure how they will respond or even if they want to be touched. If caregivers choose not to engage in positive physical touch with their teenage children, the teen will likely seek it elsewhere. They might possibly engage in physical sexual relationships earlier or seek out a boyfriend or girlfriend simply because they crave the touch. Parents can provide that loving touch to their children in a non-sexual way, protecting them from seeking out a sexual touch before they are emotionally or physically ready.

In addition to learning that touch is essential to a parent-child relationship, researchers at the University of Germany conducted

---

[17] Ellingsen, D.M., Leknes, S., Loseth, G., Wessberg, J. & Olausson, H. 1986, *The Neurobiology Shaping Affective Touch: Expectation, Motivation, and Meaning in the Multisensory Context,* Frontiers Psychology, Vol 6, Accessed August 2022, National Library of Medicine
<https://www.ncbi.nlm.nih.gov/pmc/articles/PMC4701942/>

research to find out if the same benefits of touch could be related to non-human touch such as a pet or even robotic substitutes[18]. Although they found that there were other positive benefits to touching a dog, it did not have the same neurobiological effect that human-human touch gave. This doesn't mean that guardians shouldn't encourage their children to play with and snuggle a family pet, there are great benefits from that, but there is no substitute for human to human touch.

From the information gleaned from these studies, it is clear it is the parent's job to make sure that their child is getting an abundance of positive loving touch. As shown previously, it can help lower cortisol levels, stress, and can curb aggressive behavior towards others. For this reason, we encourage caregivers to implement positive touching as much as they can. We understand that many people may not identify themselves as a "physical" or "touchy" person. This advice can especially be hard if the parent still has a young child at home. Many parents with young children get "touched out" by the end of the day and actually crave having time when they aren't being touched. When this happens, the non-caretaker spouse and other children can suffer when the mother or the primary caregiver is unable to give touch to other children and their spouse. We encourage these parents to take time for themselves as needed so that they can give some sort of loving physical affection to the other people in their household, not just the infant or toddler who requires touch as part of their caregiving. This can be done by taking an hour in the middle of the day to quietly read a book, take a nap, or watch a movie. This may sound impossible to a parent who has a lot of other demands, but if individuals can carve out a little bit of time to regenerate themselves so that they can be loving and present for the rest of the day, everyone in the household will benefit.

---

[18] Eckstein, M., Mamaev, I., Ditzen, B. & Sailer, U. 2020, *Calming Effects of Touch In HUman, Animal and Robotic Interaction- Scientific State-of-the-Art and Technical Advances.* Frontiers Psychology, Accessed August 2022, <https://www.frontiersin.org/articles/10.3389/fpsyt.2020.555058/full>

Types of Touch

Knowing how to touch a teenager in an appropriate way can be challenging for many parents. When they were young it was natural to have the child sit on a lap or carry them around on a hip, but that is no longer an option, so caregivers have to get more creative. Don't let the need for creativity discourage you from finding positive ways to love your child through touch, the benefits are so great that it is worth finding creative solutions. Here are some ideas:

Patting

One of the simplest ways to have physical connection with your child is through a gentle pat. Patting is not threatening. It is a neutral gesture and is appropriate to give to people even outside your family. You should be giving your child a loving pat multiple times throughout the day. If you are not able or comfortable giving your child a full hug, start with patting. This can be done by standing on the side of the child and simply putting your hand on the middle of their back when you address them. It might be less than 5 seconds, but it connects the two of you. You can pat their back, arm, shoulder, or knee. You can even give them a loving pat as you pass by them without saying anything. Some parents like to pat their teenage child's head. In my experience, children find that demeaning, perhaps making them feel like a small child. Also, many teenagers prefer not to have their hair fussed with. Preferably don't touch their hair or face, that can be intrusive. Stick with the shoulders, back, lower knee, or arm. The goal for all loving touch is for them to feel like they are seen and that you desire to be close to them. A simple pat takes no time on your part, but can be that very connection. Use the pat often.

Back Tickles

When my children feel unloved, back tickles are a sure way to help them feel special and comfortable. When sitting on the couch close together I will often lightly tickle their back. The majority of people find this action very pleasurable and enjoy the feeling of having their back tickled. You can do it for only a couple minutes but watch your teenage child melt into your hand as you tickle their back. If you do this, you will likely have your children coming over and ask you to tickle their back. This will happen especially during movies, reading assignments, church services, or any other time when you are sitting quietly together. When you start to get these sorts of invitations from your teens you know that you have created a safe and comfortable place for them. It also is a sign that your teen appreciates and loves comforting touch. Some children love it more than others, so keep a close eye out for a child who feels love through touch. They will benefit the most from finding ways to connect physically.

Hugs

Some families are not huggers, and that is understandable. If you didn't grow up giving hugs it can be uncomfortable or hard for you to get to a place where you feel like hugging is natural. Start small with the hugs. A side hug is an easy way to get the benefit of hugging without having to give a big bear hug. As mentioned earlier, oxytocin is released whenever you touch each other, but the best way to ensure a flood of oxytocin into the system is through a hug. Think about it, when someone is struggling, you automatically feel the need to hug them. This is an evolutionary response; our bodies know that a hug will not only help them feel supported by a friend, but it will actually create a chemical response in their body making them feel safe. Imagine the effect it would have on your child if you hugged them in the morning before they left for school, and then again after a stressful day away from you. It is like giving them a shot of stress relief medicine. A simple hug is the best way to do this. We recommend trying to give your child a hug every day if possible. But if your child is resistant to a full hug, in the beginning, start small. However, you may be surprised to see how much they positively respond to the touch. They may even start coming to you with the desire to be hugged and comforted.

Dance

Dancing has been a staple of societies for centuries. It is a natural and common way for people to have appropriate and positive touch. It can also be a great way for parents and children to connect. Many individuals talk about learning to dance with their father or mother. They relay the joy that they felt as they learned to move with the music with their parents holding their hand or the small of their back. If you are looking for a creative and fun way to connect with your child both emotionally and physically, turn on some music and swing dance, do the waltz, or polka around the room.

Sitting Close

For those who still might not feel comfortable with touch, simply sitting close together can be a great way to break the invisible barrier between your two bodies and encourage touch. When watching a family movie, just move a little closer so your shoulders are touching. This might initially take some thought on your part. You may have to make a conscious effort to just barely be touching your child. You might even find that they move away from you. That is to be expected if you are not used to touching each other. Be patient and keep trying. Over time it will become more natural for you to sit close and eventually both of you will hardly notice that your leg or shoulder is touching. Even though your conscious brain may not recognize that your bodies are touching, your chemical brain will, and it will start releasing all those happy hormones that give you a sense of well-being.

Get creative with the way you touch your child in the beginning. I promise you that if you start to implement more positive touch into your child's life you will see amazing responses. In fact, the proportion of benefit to how much you lovingly touch your teenager will feel disproportionate. You will find that a five-second hug in the morning just created hours of less fighting and a general feeling of less stress in the home. This is why caregivers and parents need to especially work on becoming more comfortable with touch with their teenage children.

Consider Barbara's experience with implementing more touch in the home:

Barbara was the mother of five children. Each one of those children was unique in their own way. Although Barbara was a competent and loving mother, she wasn't very affectionate. Touch had always been hard for her. She liked her personal space and even her husband, Richard complained that she wasn't a very touchy person. He appreciated more touch, such as hand holding, sitting close during movies, and a hug when he left and got home from work. Barbara was irritated by how much her husband and children wanted to be touched and decided that it simply wasn't for her. However, as their middle child, Kathryn, entered adolescence she was having a hard time regulating her emotions. Her main emotion was anger. Barbara and Richard were getting calls from other parents and school teachers that Kathryn was the "mean girl" and that other children were starting to avoid her. She had a biting tongue, and she was being hurtful to people she didn't like. Barbara took this seriously and knew that if she didn't intervene, Kathryn could become a bully and do emotional damage to her peers, especially to girls. After talking with some professionals about Kathryn's behavior, she was asked, "How do you show Kathryn you love her?" Barbara gave some ideas, but then was asked, "Does Kathryn do anything to show that she wants to be loved a certain way?" After thinking about it, Barbara remembered that Kathryn would often come and sit by her mom and lay her head in Barbara's lap. This was actually a major annoyance to Barbara and she believed that Kathryn was just trying to annoy her after a long day of caring for children. When this happened Barbara would usually push her off, telling her to stop. It was recommended that Barbara do two things; first accept any bid for touch that Kathryn offered, and that Barbara finds ways to show her love through touch. Although it was a challenge for Barbara, she saw startling results. At first, Kathryn didn't do much to try and touch her mom, she had been pushed away for years and she had almost stopped completely, so Barbara had to be the one to initiate it. She would give Kathryn a hug before school, she would rest her hand on Kathryn's back while they talked, and even though there was plenty of room on the couch, Barbara would sit right next to Kathryn so their shoulders and legs were touching. Within days Kathryn became almost clingy. When her mom hugged her, she would hold onto the hug longer than Barbara thought necessary. Sometimes she would sit there hugging for 20-30 seconds. Kathryn started again to put her head into her mom's lap and Barbara, rather than push her away, would gently play with Kathryn's hair or rub her back. I wish I could say that the nasty behavior at school stopped right away; it took some time and it took some hard conversations. Barbara would take the chance while they were hugging or snuggling to say things like, "I hope you are showing everyone your kindest self, everyone is fighting a silent battle you don't know about, be kind to those around, always choose kindness," etc. Over time, Kathryn softened and wasn't so aggressive. Barbara learned that her daughter desperately needed more loving touch to feel safe and secure. And since mean behavior often stems from insecurity, once Kathryn felt secure, she was less likely to treat others poorly.

Touch may not be the answer to all problems at home. It didn't solve everything for the family above, but it did help. It was an important piece of the puzzle that many teenagers are missing in their lives. Since teenagers' bodies are already flooded with cortisol and unbalanced hormones as their bodies and brains develop, it is vital that parents give them every opportunity to flood their bodies with hormones related to love and safety. This will decrease their stress response and make them feel safer. Even if caregivers don't feel like they are touchy people, like Barbara, know it may take some practice to open up to finding positive ways to have a loving physical relationship with others. Yet, the reward will exceed the effort as caregivers implement this important principle in their homes.

CHAPTER 10

What Parents Need To Know About Technology and Teenagers

We live in a world very different from what many of us grew up in. The internet, tablets, and advances in online media have become increasingly more appealing to everyone. Adults and youth alike spend massive amount of time on their phones, computers, or in front of a screen. Many schools use computers throughout the day to teach a variety of subjects and support learning. Even subjects like music that don't traditionally require computers have implemented time using technology to teach it. Computers and technology have improved the lives of many and have allowed us to have more flexibility in our work and school. It also provides a creative entertainment. However, many drawbacks have been discovered as technology has become more implemented into every second of our lives.

With the rise of technology use, specifically gaming on consoles, tablets, and phones, there has been an unusual phenomenon of individuals who show symptoms similar to those with drug addictions, but with a screen as the drug of choice. The DSM-V, which is the authority on mental health diagnoses, recently recognized that there are addictions relating to screens, gaming, cell phone, and internet use. This may seem a little far-fetched; really, a video game acting like cocaine? But first, consider what an addiction is and what it does to the brain. Addiction is a biological and chemical response in the brain. It is a learned behavior. The brain is introduced to a stimulant (substance or behavior) and over time and with repeated use of that stimulant, the brain changes so that it believes that it *needs* the stimulant to survive. It is like the brain gets confused between what is a real need and what isn't. This happens through chemical interactions. All mammals have a neurochemical called dopamine. Dopamine plays a critical role in motivation and pleasure. To determine what this vital neurochemical does, early studies looked at the effect of dopamine on the brain using rats as subjects. The study went as follows: researchers took a group of rats and taught them to press a lever; each time they pressed the lever they would receive, through electrodes, a shot of dopamine[19]. This was controlled against a group of rats who were simply taught to press the lever, but did not receive the dopamine surge. The rats who received the dopamine soon became obsessed with pressing the lever, pressing it up to a thousand times a day. The dopamine drowned rats ignored everything else, including food, sleep, and sex. Instead, they became completely focused on receiving the dopamine and nothing else. This study opened up a new field of research that explored the underlying causes of addiction. They discovered dopamine plays a critical role. Even though this information was discovered through the use of rats, we now know that this is the same for human brains. Dopamine is vital to a normal functioning brain. When certain substances are introduced or repeated pleasure-seeking behaviors become habitual, it can change the way our brain delivers and metabolizes dopamine[20].

Studies have been done on the relationship between the brain and screen use and have found similar patterns in the brain's response to technology as even those of cocaine[21]. They discovered similar rises in dopamine to the surge that a drug addict gets when they take their drug of choice. Meaning, a person playing video games, scrolling on their phone, or browsing online can feel the same pleasure that an addict gets when taking a drug. They found that the more interactive the game, or the scrolling, the more likely it is to become addictive. For example, when you are reading a hard copy of a book, you turn the page with your hand. Each time you do this your brain gives you a little

---

[19] Ask A Neuroscientist: Can Dopamine Release Become Addicting? 2014, *Wu Tsai Neuroscience Institute, Stanford University*, United States, Accessed August 2022 <https://neuroscience.stanford.edu/news/ask-neuroscientist-can-dopamine-release-become-addicting>

[20] How Does Cocaine Produce Its Effects?, 2022, *National Institute on Drug Abuse*, United States, Accessed August 2022, <https://nida.nih.gov/publications/research-reports/cocaine/how-does-cocaine-produce-its-effects>

[21] Ask A Neuroscientist: Can Dopamine Release Become Addicting? 2014, *Wu Tsai Neuroscience Institute, Stanford University*, United States, Accessed August 2022 <https://neuroscience.stanford.edu/news/ask-neuroscientist-can-dopamine-release-become-addicting>

shot of pleasure causing you to continue turning the page and not being able to set the book down. Similarly, when you read a book on your phone and you swipe right, you get that same pleasure. Imagine how much pleasure you get from simply swiping right; now compare it to the pleasure you get when playing a game, seeing something you like online, or texting with a friend. These activities are not inherently bad, but if they are done in excess and without thought and intention, they can become mindless and addictive.

In his book, "Glow Kids," Nicholas Kardaras explores the world of screen addictions[22]. He investigates mental health disorders related to excessive screen use, like depression, anxiety, psychosis, and the breakdown of healthy relationships due to too much time with technology. In his book, Kardaras emphasizes that although not every child will become addicted to screens in the traditional sense, the overuse of screens for any person, child or adult, will have negative effects on other aspects of their lives. Knowing that the overuse of screens can be dangerous is just one part of the solution. Parents need to help their teenagers actually regulate the amount of time they spend with technology. This can be incredibly hard, especially if your teenager is attached to the screen. In one instance, when the parents took away a gaming console from a child, the child was so distraught at losing his "friend" that the child required enrollment in a 12-step addiction recovery program to overcome the relationship with his gaming console [23]. This is the power of the relationship of screens for some children. Although your child may not be that severe, too much time on a screen can cause a variety of problems, including depression, anxiety, loss of friends, obesity, and social isolation[24]. Regardless, if a

---

[22] Kardaras, N. (2016) *Glow Kids: How screen addiction is hijacking our kids—and how to break the trance.* New York: St. Martin's Press.

[23] Kardaras, N. (2016) *Glow Kids: How screen addiction is hijacking our kids—and how to break the trance.* New York: St. Martin's Press.

[24] Children and Screen Time: How much is too much? 2021, *Mayo Clinic Health System,* United States, Accessed August 2022, <https://www.mayoclinichealthsystem.org/hometown-health/speaking-of-health/children-and-screen-time>

child fits the description for a full blown addiction or if they just have an unhealthy attachment to screens, parents should be intentional about how much screen time their children are allowed. Enforcing limits on screen time and technology can be challenging for both the parent and the child, especially if the habit has become out of control, but it is worth the effort and the focus. Here are some ideas for managing screen time in the home:

1. Make all family time screen-free and implement more screen-free family time. Each time you sit down for a meal, turn off the TV, and put phones away. This is for kids and parents alike. Do not let your child take food into their rooms or the common areas where games are played or phones are used. Too often busy parents allow their children to eat in front of the screen. Some kids don't even take breaks for meals or snacks. Instead, they run to the kitchen during a pause break, grab something to eat, and run back to eat it while playing a game or watching a show. This is dangerous for multiple reasons. One is that it encourages mindless eating. This can lead to overeating and ignoring the body's cues to signal when it is done. Additionally, food should be a social event with the family whenever possible. Children should have the chance to enjoy food with their parents, friends, or siblings. It is a great reminder to slow down for three meals a day and keep it social rather than technological.

2. Put time restrictions on all screen use including gaming, cell phones, social media and even texting. In our family, we have certain days when video games are allowed. On the days that they aren't allowed to play, the console is actually removed from the area. It has to be installed and set up before they can play on it. This made it more intentional for all of us. That way I couldn't use it as a babysitter when I got busy, but also that the kids knew not to ask for it on a day that wasn't video game day. Additionally, set an amount of time that they can play or use their screens, especially for browsing social media. This can

be done by installing apps on the phone that shut off the internet after a certain amount of time. Also, using timers for both parents and kids helps both of them keep track of the amount of time they spend on their phones or tablets. This is a good principle to discuss together before you set the time limits. Using the conversation cards in Chapter 4 on boundaries, you can talk with your child about what is the appropriate amount of time on a screen.

3. Use screens as a privilege, not a right or a quick solution for boredom. In the home, parents can implement a new way to think about screen time. Rather than it being a natural thing that everyone does or the preferred cure for boredom, caregivers can make it so that screens are more special. If the individual finishes their chores on time, does their homework, exercises, etc., then they can earn a certain amount of screen time. When a child feels boredom, avoid letting them immediately cure that boredom by jumping on a video game. The concern with using screens to fix boredom is that it prevents the individual from using their creative nature to find something that interests them. Boredom breeds creativity, it encourages 'out of the norm' thinking, and usually, it is when a child is bored that they will try something new. Consequently, taking away all feelings of boredom will only further isolate the teen into the screen, quash their creativity, and perhaps even their social life.

4. When you remove the screens make sure to introduce additional positive activities rather than just taking the screens away. If guardians are going to implement a severe change in the way they use screens in the home, they should be ready to replace that time with something positive. This doesn't mean that the parent needs to constantly be entertaining the kids but to soften the blow, have some activities that can be done as a family, or things teenagers enjoy. Crafts, art, music, sports, hiking, camping, cycling, etc., can all be great replacements.

5. Keep all charging stations for phones, computers, tablets, and electronics outside of their bedroom. Decide on a time each night that the family will put away technology. They should never be taking these devices to their rooms. This is a breeding ground for not only time wasting, but dangerous online activities. Protect their sleep and protect their downtime by never allowing these devices in their room at bedtime.

It is important for parents to realize that they are not alone in the war against technology enveloping our children. It is something that every home has to address, and if caregivers don't intentionally make a plan of how they will handle screens, others will make a plan for them; and that plan will take over their lives. Here is Carol's story of how technology affected her children:

Carol is a loving mother of three children. She came to me worried about her children's mental health. All three of her children had different levels of depression and anxiety. She saw all of them struggling in their own individual way, and even though she was concerned about it, she kept assuming it would get better. Finally, it wasn't until her oldest son, Lucas, turned 16 did she decide to seek help. When Lucas was a child, he would talk excitedly about when he would turn 16. He was excited to get his driver's license, begin dating, and have the freedom to spend more time with friends. Carol expected by 16 he would begin to have some idea of his interests and possible professions, but none of this happened. At 16, Lucas was withdrawn, disinterested in friends, school, and dating. He got his driver's license, but only because his parents made him. Carol was concerned that her other two children, a boy and a girl, were on track for the same problems. Even when her kids received social invitations, they all felt nervous to be with others and isolated themselves. Before really getting into possible resources specifically for anxiety, I asked questions that could help me better understand their home life. Carol didn't mention anything out of the norm, but when I visited with Lucas he told me that after school he would come home, finish his homework, and then jump on his favorite video game, Fortnite. He told me that the people he considered his best friends were gaming friends that he had met online. He had never actually met them in person. He said that he played Fortnite from the time he finished his homework at 3:00 p.m. till he went to bed at night, which would be sometime between 11:00 and midnight. Even with taking small breaks for food and the bathroom, he would be playing as much as 7-8 hours a day. That is the same amount of time he was at school or what most of us would consider a full-time job. This didn't even account for the time that he would play on the weekends. He mentioned he sometimes would play on the weekends through the night on Saturday, sleep in late on Sunday, and then jump back on. When Carol visited with me, Lucas sat behind her scrolling on his phone. He rarely made eye contact and seemed uncomfortable talking to me. Unfortunately, for Lucas, I saw some red flags right away. This child was so deep into screens that much of the depression and anxiety were attributed to his lack of balance. The first thing Carol was assigned to do with this child was to take away the screens-cold turkey. This was incredibly hard on their family because it wasn't only Lucas that enjoyed the screens. His siblings loved them (they all had their own console so they could play without waiting turns,) and the younger children also spent hours a day gaming or on their smartphones. Carol was tasked to find other activities to replace gaming. First, she signed them up for sports and in some cases had to drag them along. She took them to museums and zoos. It should be mentioned that they complained the whole time. She set up filters on their phones, which they did their darndest to get around. Luckily, Carol understood that fighting screens would take time and that her children would need patience through this painful adjustment. After about a month, she started to see improvement. They still asked for screens every day, sometimes multiple times a day, but their mental health began to improve. All of the kids felt less social anxiety and depression. It was only after removing this underlying problem with technology that we could see where the depression started and where the effects of the technology ended.

If this story seems severe to many, they might want to take a realistic inventory of their relationship to technology. For many parents, they think, "My child only spends 'x' amount of time on their phone, gaming console, tablet, etc." But parents need to take a good hard look at how much technology their teenage children are really using. Carol was shocked to learn how many hours her kids were playing on consoles or spending on their phones once we really added it all up. Several parents routinely check their children's phones to see how much time they spend on it. Many devices, such as the iPhone, keep track of the amount of time you spend on the device and which apps you are using. Caregivers should also be checking their child's text messaging to see whom they message, at what time of day, and how often. Guardians may be surprised to learn that their child is texting, playing games, and scrolling the internet when they are at school, with their friends, or even at night when they should be sleeping. We as parents also need to hold up a mirror to ourselves and be realistic about the amount of time we spend on our devices. We can start by being an example to put down our phones and really interact with those around us.

In addition to the mental health challenges that overuse of technology can cause, caregivers also need to be aware of the dangers of unsupervised internet use. According to Kaspersky Lab, cyber predators, relating to human trafficking and exploitation of children, are a severe problem that is on the rise[25]. A teenage child's brain is not able to fully understand the long-term risks and dangers of posting pictures of themselves online, or conversing with strangers. Teenagers and young children are being lured into dangerous situations where their safety is compromised. This happens most often through social media apps, chat rooms, and online gaming platforms. It cannot be stressed enough that guardians must be aware of what their children

---

[25] Internet Safety For Kids: How To Protect Your Child From The Top 7 Dangers They Face Online, 2022, Kaspersky Lab. Accessed September 2022, United States. <https://usa.kaspersky.com/resource-center/threats/top-seven-dangers-children-face-online>

are doing online and ensure that the child is educated about the dangers that potentially await them.

In relation to social media and internet use, Wait Until 8th, a movement for delaying smartphone use until 8th grade, and social media apps until 16 years of age, have made it their mission to protect children online[26]. Before giving children a cellphone and unfettered access to the world wide web, parents should make a very conscious and calculated decision about the right time for their child. For many children, they are not mature enough even at 8th grade for a phone. In our home, we don't allow personal social media accounts until after high school graduation. Additionally, after the child has a phone or these accounts, parents should be checking in often to see what they are posting, who they are talking to, and be on alert for any dangerous behavior.

As guardians make these challenging changes in their family to put a limit on screens and technology, it may be painful, but be assured, it is worth it. In Chapter 4 you will find conversation starters about technology specifically. It will help to soften the shock if parents talk about the changes they are going to make before they try to implement them. This will ensure that everyone in the family understands what is going on and the consequences for everyone, mom and dad included, if these rules are broken.

---

[26] Why Wait? Wait Until 8th. 2022, Accessed September 2022, United States <https://www.waituntil8th.org/why-wait>

CHAPTER 11

Addressing Anxiety, Depression & Mental Illness

It is estimated that as many as 1 in 5 teenagers deal with depression during their adolescent years[27]. Of those who suffer from depression, only 30% of them receive any treatment for it. Unfortunately, 1 in 3 teenagers suffer from anxiety during their adolescent years. For 10% of those individuals, it will be so debilitating that they will be unable to complete normal tasks, go to school, or be able to function socially with their peers[28]. With these startling statistics, it shouldn't be surprising to guardians when children suffer from depression, anxiety, or other mental illness. Parents of multiple children should recognize that it is statistically likely that at least one of their children will be diagnosed with mental illness. Educators, legislators and parents alike wonder why the increase in these disorders. Causes are unknown, but we do know that genetics, environment, increasing demands on time, chemical exposure, and personality play a role. Knowing that their child has a high chance of confronting a mental illness at some point in their teenage years can prepare parents to know how to help.

Treatment

Unfortunately, even though many people suffer from mental illnesses, a staggeringly low number of those individuals actually get treatment for it. This is sadly due to perceptions about mental illness, embarrassment, and a lack of education. Too many people feel that their child's anxiety and/or depression are a reflection on them as parents. Because of this, they avoid seeking mental health professionals, and instead, encourage their child to snap out of it. It is unlikely that a child will be able to simply change the way their mind thinks simply because their caregiver told them to. Regrettably, too many people don't understand how anxiety and depression work. They

[27] Depression Symptoms In Teens: Why Todays Teen's Are More Depressed Than Ever, 2016, *Discovery Mood & Anxiety Program*, United States, Accessed August 2022, <https://discoverymood.com/blog/todays-teens-depressed-ever/>
[28] Teen Stress and Anxiety: Facts and Statistics, 2022, *Evolve Treatment Centers*, United States, Accessed August 2022, <https://discoverymood.com/blog/todays-teens-depressed-ever/>

believe that it can be solved with positive thinking. Although positive thinking is critical, this alone cannot fix all anxiety or depression. When trying to understand why a person's mind continually goes to depressive or anxious thoughts, consider this example:

A hiker in the mountains comes across two paths. Both of the trails will lead them to their destination. They do not know that the trail to the right is faster, safer, and easier. For a reason unbeknownst to them, they choose the path on the left. The hiker then takes this trail every day, even multiple times a day. Over time the trail on the left begins to become well worn. This trail becomes the preferred and only trail the hiker will take; it has become automatic to him. Each time he walks this mountain he is on autopilot and always chooses the path to the left. Over time the path to the right, which has rarely if ever been used, becomes overgrown. Therefore, it is less likely that the hiker will ever choose the right side.

In this metaphor, the mountain is like your brain. The hiker is your neural wiring. The more you take the trail on the left, the more skilled your brain becomes at going that way. It might become the preferred and only way you go. This is how addictions are formed. This is how bad habits are created. Soon without even thinking about it, you are doing certain things or behaving a certain way. You might not know any other way than to take the path on the left. In this example, the path represents maladaptive coping mechanisms or bad habits. This is what causes you stress, fear, panic attacks, worry, and so forth. The path to the right is actually better, but you will have to reteach your neural hiker to take that better path. Through therapy and proper training, you can retrain or rewire your brain to take this new path. Imagine that the first few times this hiker takes the trail to the right, it is painful; it is awkward, there are trees, it is rough with rocks, and it feels like a ton of work. Then over time it becomes easier. Each time the hiker chooses the path to the right, his feet begin to pound down the dirt. The trail becomes more worn and easier to use. Conversely, the trail to the left (also known as the maladaptive and unhealthy trail) has now become undesirable and unused.

Initially when an individual starts to retrain their brain, or to use the example above, walks on the new trail, it will feel strange and even silly. Many times in treatment, the person will do such simple exercises that it will be hard to trust that something as simple as saying the feeling aloud or doing a circle of control worksheet, could actually combat such overwhelming feelings of depression or anxiety. However, it is amazing what the human brain is capable of doing. It is a muscle, and just like any other muscle in the body if it is exercised a certain way it will become stronger. Treatment for anxiety and depression will look different for everyone, but here are some options that work for many individuals:

Therapy & Counseling

Therapy and counseling can be incredibly effective in dealing with anxiety and depression. Just like in the metaphor with the hiker, the counselor essentially teaches the person how to take the better path with their thoughts. For example, if their learned reaction to certain stressors is panic, they can help the person train their brain not to immediately take the path of panic. For example, your child might be struggling with panic in social situations. Each time they encounter a new person they need to "small talk" with, they have a panic attack and want to leave. Over time this causes them to avoid almost all social situations. In this case, the counselor might help them to practice some calming tools as well as give them conversational tools that they can use when they enter social situations. Initially, it will be hard and awkward as your child tries to enter an uncomfortable social scene, but once it goes well, their brain has had its first successful walk down the new path. As these skills continue to be practiced, the panic will subside, and it will get easier. The counselor will teach them how to be mindful of their emotions without believing that their emotions control them. They will learn grounding techniques, calming breathing, and other skills that can combat the intense feelings of emotions.

If you choose to do counseling with your child, it is important that you are supportive as well. Counseling requires that the patient trust the professional. Too many times I have encountered caregivers who tried a session or two of counseling with their child and scoffed at the seemingly simplicity of the tasks they were asked to do. For some, the simplicity of the directions are almost offensive to the guardians. They went to counseling with the hope that the counselor would have some sort of magic pill, or life changing advice that will solve the problem quickly. Unfortunately, the best results come from the simple acts done consistently and with intention. If the parent isn't "all in" in trying what is asked, then you can be sure the child is going to follow the parent's lead. In situations where you don't know what to do, trust the professionals who have seen this hundreds of times, and try to have the humility needed to do the simple things.

When doing any treatment plan, consistency is key. You need to be implementing any home program or homework on your own. Encourage your child to do the exercises at home. Familiarize yourself with the treatment program so that you can get the most benefit. Merely seeing a counselor for one hour a week won't transform your life unless you are using the skills at home each day.

Medication & Supplements

Pharmacological treatment can bring amazing benefits to individuals when they are prescribed and administered properly. When trying to understand what medication can do for your teen, let's go back to the hiker metaphor. Many times the reason the hiker is taking the same route is because they are tired. They can hardly move, their body is fatigued, and imagine they don't have enough nutrients or water. Of course, they are going to take the path of least resistance to get to their destination. Conversely, there are some instances where the hiker is so energized that even if you told them to go a different way they would be unable to. They won't listen or slow down long enough to even think about where they are going. If you are going to ask the hiker to change routes and take the harder path, you need the hiker to be functioning at optimal levels. It is vital that this hiker be able to complete tasks as told and that their body is functioning properly.

Like the hiker, with anxiety and depression, the neural networks aren't working on the right level. For some, the neural networks are too weak and slow. In other cases, the mind can't slow down enough so that the brain can make changes. Instead, it is in a survival mode where it chooses the most used and easiest neural path. In both of these cases, medication helps to balance the neural chemicals so that the brain has the energy and focus it needs to think properly. Some of these chemicals include serotonin, dopamine, glutamate, and GABA. When any of these neural chemicals are not functioning properly, you will likely suffer a loss of motivation, limited focus, no pleasure in activities, destructive thought loops, and more. Think of medication as giving the hiker food, water, and a compass.

Additionally, guardians can explore vitamins and supplements. Vitamins play a vital role in metabolizing nutrients and healthy functioning. You might all have the nutrients your body needs, but without the proper vitamins, you cannot metabolize them correctly. This is why many professionals recommend changing your diet, taking supplements, and looking closely at the foods that you are eating. For some, introducing a synthetic neurochemical, like a controlled substance, isn't necessary. They have plenty of neurochemicals in their body, what they lack is the vitamins to properly use those nutrients and chemicals. Some parents prefer to start with diet and vitamins rather than medication. This can help to determine if vitamins are the reason your neural hiker is fatigued and unable to perform. Talk to your child's doctor or dietitian to determine if your child could benefit from a diet change or a vitamin supplement.

If your child has clinical depression or anxiety, meaning that it isn't just a "bad day" or situational, it is likely that the neural chemicals aren't balanced or working properly, and therapy alone may not be enough. Most parents find that a combination of the two will be the best way to see progress. In some cases, you can push therapy, but if the neurochemicals are unbalanced, the progress will be limited because those hikers, or neural connections, are unable to listen and make the changes needed to see progress. If your child is dealing with depression or anxiety, and it has become debilitating, or if they are resistant to making changes, consider talking to their doctor about medication. For many teenagers, medication and/or vitamin supplements are safe and effective options.

Capacity & Choice

One of the hardest things for parents and loved ones of those dealing with depression, anxiety, and mental illness is understanding how much capacity the individual has. When a person is dealing with depression or anxiety, they might say "I can't do…" and as a parent, your first instinct may be asking, "You can't, or you won't?" There is some validity to this question. Depression and anxiety affect dopamine which can influence motivation. So even though they are physically able to do something they may emotionally feel like it is impossible. This is especially the case with schoolwork, housework, or participating in family activities. As the child gets older, if they are depressed, they may become more resistant to participating in activities that they once enjoyed. For younger children, such as preteen and younger, depression and anxiety usually manifest in whining, excessive crying, agitation, separation anxiety, fear of parent leaving, and sickness (like stomach aches and headaches). For teenagers, the manifestations can be similar, but included should also be resistance to parents, over-sleeping, avoiding friends and social situations, and fighting with parents and siblings. As explained, caregivers might wonder which of these manifestations the child has control over. Do they sleep too much because they are so fatigued that they can't get out of bed? Or do they sleep too much because their parents aren't forcing them to get up and face life? If the first were true and they didn't have the capacity, you would be compassionate, seek out medical treatment, and try to lovingly encourage the child to get the help they need. In the second case, you might punish them for being disrespectful and ignoring the order to get out of bed and get their chores done. Unfortunately, there is no clear answer on where the choice begins and capacity ends. Additionally, it will be different for each person. What might be a choice for one individual to ignore their schoolwork because they have no motivation, might be a capacity issue for another individual who cannot mentally focus on the schoolwork even with their best intentions.

Although you cannot solve this problem and be the all-knowing eye of what is going on in your child's head, there are some things that you can do to encourage empathy when that is needed, and tough love when that is required. Here are some suggestions:

1) Have open conversations with your child about how they are feeling. Try not to be too pushy initially. Most likely the child doesn't even understand what they are feeling. They might not be able to express it so you may have to label the emotion for them. For example:

Hannah was 14 years old and was a fun loving and energetic child. But as she entered her teenage years, she increasingly became more somber. Often, she would come back from her favorite activities like soccer and track and cry in the car on the way home. These were always very quiet, silent tears, not sobs, but still, her mother was concerned. When Kathy, Hannah's mom, would ask Hannah why she was crying, Hannah would simply shrug her shoulders. Initially, Kathy thought that Hannah was just blowing her off when she would shrug and say I don't know, but after gently prying, Kathy learned that Hannah really *didn't* know why she was crying. Hannah had a hard time expressing complex emotions as it was and all she knew was that she felt like crying. Kathy decided to try to help Hannah label her emotions. She started by asking, "Are you still enjoying soccer?" Hannah responded yes. "Are you still enjoying track?" Once again yes. "Do you want to take a break from sports?" Hannah responded, no. As they went through gentle questioning like this, Kathy went from sports to friends, friends to school work, school work to home life, and so forth. While asking questions, both Hannah and Kathy discovered what was troubling Hannah. Hannah felt like she was changing and she didn't enjoy her childhood friends as much as she used to. They were able to label the feeling as guilt. Hannah felt like she should still want to be with the friends she had before, but now she was bonding more with the girls on her sports team. Rather than this thought making her happy, she felt sad and guilty that this would mean she would have to choose between the two friend groups. Once Kathy knew this, she and Hannah could begin working together to decide how Hannah could keep both friend groups without hurting anyone and how Hannah could find a balance that worked for her.

As you can see in the example, Hannah knew she felt sad, but she didn't know why. Depression and anxiety are often like this. Even though Hannah had a reason for feeling down, her reaction was severe to the situation. This was a red flag to her mom that she might be dealing with depression because Hannah's emotions were strong and her moods were generally low. Kathy was able to watch Hannah closely to make sure that her reactions were appropriate. If it became a prolonged issue, they would explore options for treating Hannah's disproportional low moods.

2) Allow set times for moping and then encourage, even force them, to move on. When your child is in a mood and they simply won't comply, you can put boundaries on the child that are helpful for both parent and child. It gives you both reasonable expectations of what the individual will do. Consider this example, your son is sulking in his room and refuses to come out to a family party. You might say, "You have 20 minutes to take the time that you need. Get your bearings and recharge. Then in 20 minutes, you're going to come out and give me what I need." When you do this make sure it isn't a threat or punishment. It is an exchange or a compromise. You don't say, "You have 20 minutes to pull yourself together and stop acting so dramatically!" This only fuels the fire and makes the child feel defensive. Rather than help, you will cause them to feel like they need to prove that they are not dramatic. They might spend all the time they could be using to recharge, trying to convince you that they are in pain. It will escalate quickly. Instead, validate them by telling them, "Yes, I know this is hard for you, that is why I am going to give you space for a time. But once that time is over, you need to come and do this for

me." Many times, this will help you determine if the child has the capacity to do what you ask.

3) Be their crutch when they need it, but let them know that eventually, they will need to walk alone. As you go through this difficult journey with your child, it is important that you don't abandon them. They really might need extra help. Just like a child learning to walk, you will need to hold their hand. This can be hard for many parents because depression and anxiety can hit unexpectedly and things that your child once did on their own now require your help. You may have to sit and do schoolwork with them, hang out in the car while they go to a birthday party just so that they know you are out there, and so forth. For many caregivers whose children suffer from depression and anxiety, they feel confused because most teenagers want more independence, not more time with their parents. If your child is dealing with anxiety, they may want you around them being their emotional support all the time. This is exhausting and rough for the parent. However, simply pushing them out the door, and telling them to figure it out, may not always work. Use your intuition. For a while, you can help your child learn to walk, but eventually, when you see that they are ready, start to give them more space and teach them to trust themselves. This may be a painful process for both parents and teens. If you find that you are having a hard time knowing when you should help and when to let go, talk to a counselor. They will be able to look at your parent-child relationship and give you some helpful insight that you may not be able to see yourself.

It is not possible in one chapter to cover everything that you need to know about mental illness and your teenager. Hopefully, this chapter has given you a small introduction to some things that you should be aware of and inspire you to take your child's mental health seriously. At any point, if you are worried about your child's mental health, you should reach out to professionals and seek additional resources.

CHAPTER 12

Becoming A Safe Haven for Your Teen

As caregivers try to implement different techniques in their homes, they will find that some work and some don't. However, one final place all parents should give attention to is creating safe places for their children, especially as they enter the tumultuous pre-teen and teen years. When a toddler is learning to walk and exploring the world, guardians take measures to place safety features around the house. They gate the stairs until they learn to crawl down them and they add child safe locks to doors that house cleaning supplies and dangerous chemicals they can ingest; to put it simply, most guardians went through the houses, looked at every possible way their child could get hurt and they created a safety plan. As a child grows up, those safety features are removed and they are allowed more independence and trust. Although a teenage child is no longer in need of protection from things like stairs, accidental ingestion, and sharp corners; the things that will most likely harm them are emotional. Even though there is no safety lock on their emotions, parents can create a home that is an emotionally safe place for their children.

Child psychologist Kim J. Payne has observed that children and teens of the past 20 years are displaying similar symptoms to children in other countries who have suffered wartime Post Traumatic Stress Disorder or PTSD[29]. He observed that children and teens who came into his practice displayed behaviors such as anxiety, depression, feelings of hopelessness, and a learned helplessness. Their emotions were unregulated and they didn't understand how to manage the complex feelings they were having about the world around them. He postulated that this was due to an overabundance of activities, entertainment, and stress surrounding their lives. He also noticed that these children were involved in too many "adult" conversations, especially those about the news, current events, tragedies in the world, and complex social situations. These topics are heavy even for adults to handle, let alone children.

---

[29] Payne, K.J. & Ross, L.M., (2009). *Simplicity Parenting*. New York: Ballantine Books.

PTSD is a serious mental disorder that is an intense response to trauma. Some children and teens do in fact have PTSD, and need clinical help to overcome it. However, the thing that many individuals do not understand is that some people show similar symptoms to PTSD from seemingly small traumas in their lives. Yes, a child who has been through a large traumatic event, like the death of a parent, a car accident, house fire, or abuse, will most surely suffer from the after effects. But someone could also develop PTSD-like symptoms from repeated small traumas that add up together. These small traumas can be mistreatment at school, a parent or teacher who is constantly belittling or nagging them, and essentially anything that the child sees as threatening could cause symptoms like PTSD. I am not suggesting that all children or even a majority have PTSD. Yet, I hope to impress upon parents that our children may be experiencing stressors that they don't know how to handle. Thus, they are reverting to negative coping strategies as they learn to navigate the world around them.

Parents can help to combat these unhealthy coping strategies that their teens may adopt. Although caregivers can't control the environment and aren't able to fix every negative interaction they have with a peer, the good news is, they don't have to. As a child ages, learning to handle unpleasant things in their environment is normal for development and progression. In fact, guardians should allow their child to experience these things, so long as they are physically safe and there is no serious mistreatment (i.e., bullying, abuse) happening. They will gain confidence as they learn how to work with difficult people, navigate friend drama, and work towards better communication. But, just because the parent can't fix it doesn't mean they shouldn't be present. Hopefully, in the process, the teen will see their parents as their biggest supporter and cheerleader.

To illustrate this concept, consider boxing. In boxing, the fighter is in the ring, and they will be in the ring alone. Everyone knows that the athlete will deliver a few punches, but they will also take some hard blows. During the sport, there is a cornerman there watching, coaching, and giving help and encouragement. This cornerman doesn't step into the ring with the fighter, that is not allowed. If they do get into the ring, both the fighter and the cornerman would be disqualified, yet the cornerman is there every step of the way.

As a teenager gains more independence, caregivers will have to allow them to enter the ring. They will learn to take the punches of life and they will learn how they can best defend themselves. But does that mean that parents wash their hands and say, "I am done with raising them; they are on their own!" Some parents, in their frustration over their teen's new independence and his or her seemingly disinterest in familiar relationships, check out for the teen years. They silently watch from the bleachers, hoping for the best. Try to avoid this. Instead, the transition from childhood to adulthood, called adolescence, is not the time for caregivers to completely leave the ring, but instead take the role of the cornerman. Stand at the side, actively watch, and then jump in when possible to give encouragement, advice, and help when needed.

Initially, a teenage child may not be open to advice if the parent has not had an active role up to this point. They might feel like the advice is nagging. Many parents assume that being the corner man means more advice than encouragement. Yes, caregivers can see things their child needs to fix, but if the relationship is at a point where giving advice causes friction, pull back and give encouragement. In fact, even if the child is open to conversation, remember guardians should be giving more encouraging remarks to their child than critiques or critical observations. For any questions, refer back to Chapter 3. Doing this will protect their self-esteem. If caregivers build a foundation of trust, it will make the advice more well received. Giving encouragement and love will also make the home a safe place.

A Safe Home Life

Making the home a safe place might be one of the most important things parents can implement. Focus on making the home a safe environment where teens can decompress from growing up and life's stresses; a place they feel like they are just that, *home*. Many times, caregivers believe that making their child feel at home means giving them everything they want or allowing them to just chill. Yes, part of feeling at home is being able to relax and parents should allow ample opportunity for unstructured time where they can choose to do an activity that is relaxing to them; but it is so much more than that. Home can be a place where they can let down their emotions. This may not always look positive. For example, a mother may find that her teenage daughter comes home and cries for a bit after a hard day at school. Don't discourage those tears, instead, help her process those emotions and let her cry and talk through them. A son or daughter may not cry, although many boys do and should be allowed to if that is their preferred way to process, instead, they may feel fidgety; so, jumping on a tramp, going for a walk with a parent while they talk, or simply being together in quiet comfort, can be healing to them. A home is a place where they can show their most vulnerable selves; where they can show their worst self and still be loved. This doesn't mean that when they show their worst selves guardians simply accept it and let them act or treat others in the house badly. It means that when they come at their worst, mom or dad shows up and sticks with them while they help them become their best. In fact, being able to show every part of themselves, both the good and the bad, while having a parent love them through it can do wonders for their feelings of self-worth.

Brene Brown, a prominent psychologist who has done extensive research on shame, has discovered that feelings of shame prevent individuals from fully accepting who they are and embracing both the flaws as well as the good things[30]. Teenagers are especially prone to feelings of shame, even when what they're doing isn't shameful. They are so concerned with fitting in, or being liked, that they feel as though they need to hide things about themselves in fear of being "discovered." The parent's job is to help them work through those concerns and feelings of shame and show them that every part of

---

[30] Shame vs. Guilt, 2013, *Brene Brown*, United States, Accessed August 2022, <https://brenebrown.com/articles/2013/01/15/shame-v-guilt/>

themselves is loved and accepted. Brene Brown said, "If you put shame in a Petri dish, it needs three ingredients to grow exponentially: secrecy, silence, and judgment. If you put the same amount of shame in the Petri dish and douse it with empathy, it can't survive."[31] It is the caregiver's job to show empathy and love to their child. This doesn't mean that parents will condone their bad behavior. The goal is to help them rid themselves of bad behavior. The difference between causing them to feel shame or hope in overcoming the undesirable behavior is *how* you deal with it. Consider this example:

Rosa was a devoted and caring mother to Daniel. Daniel was normally an outgoing, fun-loving kid. He always had friends around him. During his middle school years, Daniel started using language that Rosa and her husband Robert found offensive. Since Daniel had younger siblings, his parents didn't want that language used in their house, but even more, they didn't want their son using that language *anywhere*. Initially, when Daniel started using this language, Rosa responded with, "We don't use that type of language in our house, don't say it again." When the problem continued, Robert and Rosa decided that this was a time to show Daniel that he was seen, but also figure out *why* he was using this language. Rather than punish him immediately or get into big arguments with Daniel, which was common for both Rosa and Robert, they decided to take time to talk to Daniel more. Robert invited Daniel to go for walks together in the evenings after dinner. To help encourage Daniel to go on the walk he was given the option to stay and do the dishes or go on a walk with mom or dad. He usually chose the walk. Rosa also got in the habit of turning off the music in the car while she drove Daniel to and from activities which would encourage conversation. During these talks, Rosa and Robert used examples given in Chapter 4 for conversation starters, to get Daniel talking about his friends and his social life. They learned that Daniel was trying hard to fit in. He had friends he really enjoyed being around, but these friends used terrible language. In the

---

[31] Brown, B. (2018). *Dare to lead.* London, England: Vermilion.

beginning, it made him feel uncomfortable, but he liked being included and felt older and more mature when he used this language. Even though he knew it was offensive, he felt that fitting in with his friends was more important than following a family rule. Through these talks, Daniel shared insecurities with his parents, things about his friends that he worried about, but also things he enjoyed doing. Instead of immediately shutting him down and telling Daniel that his friends weren't right for him, Rosa and Robert listened and loved. Eventually they gave counsel and support to help him find a way to maintain positive friendships without compromising their family morals by using offensive language.

Teenagers are going to do stupid things, and many times when they do these things, they know that they have crossed a line and they feel shame, worry, and panic that they either won't be accepted by their peers or loved by their parents. As parents, we need to avoid the knee-jerk reaction of flying off the handle with our teenagers. They are emotional enough; they fly off the handle at the smallest provocation. We can emulate emotional self control as we avoid making them feel shame for trying to learn how to grow up. When we do this, we give our children a safe place to communicate with us, a place where they know that they can go to mom and dad about anything, embarrassing, or simply silly. As they deal with navigating friends and compromising moral situations, they will feel comfortable talking to us about it because even when they did something dumb, they knew that their mom or dad had their back. Safety comes from all small acts of empathy, love, and acceptance for our teenagers.

A Note from The Author on Forgiving Ourselves and Setting Realistic Goals

Years ago, I was reading a parenting book and thinking, "This is so unrealistic! This man must not have children because there is no way that this could possibly be a reality." In fact, it seemed the writer was working more with robots than human beings because the information made it sound like, if you do X then your child will react by doing Y. The reality of parenthood is that you are not dealing with robots; you have living, breathing, individual children who have a divine gift of free will. They get to choose who they want to be, and who they will become. You might do X and get a result of Z, A, G, F, and everything else in between. To complicate matters, even more, it could change from day to day or week to week how your child reacts to different parenting. While reading this book, I bet you probably wondered, "What are her five children like? Are they the perfect models of behavior, obedience, and friendship?" The short answer is, no.

They are fantastic kids and we strive constantly for more peace in the home through intentional parenting, but even in the best of circumstances, we fall short. Our kids do things we don't approve of and my husband and I try not to blame ourselves for their failures. This book is not designed to make parents feel guilt, or conversely, encourage the false belief that you can control your children. Instead, the goal is always to strive for the ideal. You can strive for the ideal home life by implementing intentional parenting techniques into everyday life, fully knowing that it won't be perfect. There will be no perfect outcomes. However, I can assure you that if you strive for the ideal and even make marginal improvements, your overall home life and the life of your children will improve. It may not be the "quick fix" or a magic pill, but it will improve.

Here are some helpful suggestions if you are dealing with feelings of failure as a parent:

Performance Goals vs. Becoming Goals

As mentioned in Chapter 6, parents can put their focus on either performance goals or learning goals. This is not only helpful for the mental health and self-esteem of the child, but it is also helpful for the parent too. Scott Kaufmann explains that when we focus on learning, we are more likely to feel successful[32]. If we are constantly setting ourselves up to only see worthiness by our performance, we will come up short. As parents, we often look at our children's achievements as a measurement of our parenting. We might feel that a child's good grades, number of friends, or athletic and musical ability are a good measurement of how we are doing as a parent. This is a dangerous mindset because it minimizes the reality of what makes a person healthy and kind. When asked, most parents would likely prefer a child who is kind, respectful, and happy over a child who has many achievements. Yet, we parents put a great deal of emphasis on the performance of our children. When measuring the success of your parenting, and your child, look for the good and recognize the progress, not the achievements.

Hard Things Make Us Better

No parent would intentionally put their children in challenging situations to "teach them a lesson," yet, growth comes from discomfort and even making mistakes. Remember the mistakes that you made in your youth and the lessons you learned from them? Perhaps you had a group of friends that was hard and brought out the worst in you. Over time, those experiences and what you learned from those friends encouraged you to choose a different lifestyle and gave you invaluable life experience. Maybe you were a hard teenager for your parents, and through that, you learned the importance of respect and appreciation. Although you would prefer your child's life to be carefree and smooth sailing, if it isn't, know that your child is having experiences that will likely help them become a better person in the long run.

---

[32] Kaufman, S.B. (2013) *Ungifted: Intelligence Redefined.* Philadelphia, PA: Basic Books

Focus On the Long-Term

Along with the suggestions above, perspective is everything as a parent. Many mothers could tell you that when they were new moms, they would often get stopped and told by older women to "enjoy these days," or "it goes by in a blink," and so forth. In some cases, a sleep deprived mom might have felt frustrated at the comment, but now looking back on raising your children, you probably feel similarly. They were right, it does go by fast, and you find yourself missing those things about the early days of your child's life. The people who can find the most joy and avoid anxiety about parenting are those who can remove themselves from the emotional here and now, and instead view their current situation with maturity and perspective.

Put Yourself in Your Child's Shoes

Empathy is said to be the key to all human relationships. If you can have empathy for the people around you, you will have strong and loyal friends for the rest of your life. Many times we view our children as "having it all" or "getting everything we never had." It is natural for us to want to give our children everything, but it can also make us unsympathetic when they feel sad or frustrated. We can't imagine what they would be sad about. If you can put yourself in their shoes, it will help you feel less frustrated. As a young mother, I took my infant daughter, only 6 months at the time, to a concert. I was looking forward to spending an evening outside the home, and we had no one to watch our child. The concert was family friendly, and I assumed my daughter would sleep or rest peacefully in my arms. Boy, was I wrong! She hated the whole evening and since we were there with a group of friends, I wasn't able to leave and take her home. Instead, I stood in the hallway trying to keep her quiet. I was privately feeling sorry for myself and frustrated with her. It was then that an older woman stopped to talk to me. She said, "Can you imagine how frustrating it is to be a baby? I wonder what they are trying to communicate and we as parents just don't get it? She seems to have such a big personality and must be so annoyed she can't express herself!" This sentiment hit me like a ton of bricks. I had never stopped to consider that my daughter might have a reason for acting difficult. I assumed she selfishly was just trying to make me miserable. When I was able to step back and be sympathetic to her situation, I felt more love, patience, and understanding. Eventually, this daughter grew up and now, we go to concerts together. The frustration was short-lived for both of us. I am so grateful for the kind woman who helped me have more perspective and empathy towards my child.

Look For the Good

One of the most frustrating things about parenting is that you can't mold your child into who *you* want them to be. Children come with a God-given personality and although you can help them to mold it, you cannot change the core part of who they are. Consider this example:

Sandra was a serious woman who valued sober mindedness. She was a professional business woman and her husband was an attorney. Together they appreciated classical music, intellectual conversation, and were structured people. When their son Bradley was born they could tell he was a fun loving kid. To him, everything was about having fun. As he grew older, they saw that he loved making people laugh. He would read joke books and try out his jokes on strangers, family members, neighbors, and practically anyone who would listen to him. And in the beginning, it was hard to listen. His jokes were awkward, and his pre-teen humor was fun for him but very few others. Initially, Sandra tried to parent the light mindedness out of Bradley. She felt that the frivolity and love for comedy weren't valuable. She never imagined that her son would be so different from her and her husband. Over time, as she tried to change Bradley, it became a problem for both her and him. He felt bad about himself, and she felt frustrated and guilty for making him feel insecure. It wasn't until Sandra branched out of her shell and started to read about different comedians and their childhoods could she appreciate Bradley's love for comedy. It has been unnatural for her, but she knows it is *natural for him* and she honors that about her son. Now, rather than constantly trying to change this part of Bradley, she embraces it and allows him to explore comedy. She even helps to find resources for him to make his jokes more applicable.

Like Sandra, we have children that may not fit our idea of what our children or family would look like. We may have believed we would have athletic children, only to have a child who loves reading. We have children who are dramatic and we are not. This doesn't mean that you need to change your child; if you try too much, it will make them feel bad about themselves. First, start by embracing who they are and loving them for it, and in spite of it. Then as the relationship progresses you can help them branch out if it feels appropriate. There is good in every individual. Focus on the good when times get hard.

Respect the Free Will of Your Child

When it comes down to it, we have to understand that our children will make their own decisions. Although we can be guides and helpers, we cannot control them. In past decades parents used to say, "I don't know what is wrong with him!" when their child would act up. Now they say, "I don't know what is wrong with *me!*" This type of thinking can be dangerous because it gives us parents a false idea that we can control the outcome for our children. Every good thing your child does is not a reflection of you and also every bad thing your child does is not a reflection of you. Instead, it is a complicated mix of so many factors and parents must be able to remove themselves enough to respect their child's free will when they make a choice that is different from what they want for them. This will only get harder as you parent adult children. The teenage years are the first real dose of understanding just how individual our children are.

Chapter 3, and the study on rabbits, explains that kindness is one of the most influential attributes of a person[33]. When we get into complicated situations while parenting, it is important to show ourselves the same amount of kindness we show to our children. By

---

[33] Harding, K. (2019). *The Rabbit Effect: Live Longer, Happier and Healthier With The Groundbreaking Science of Kindness.* New York: Atria Books.

doing this we can forgive ourselves when we make mistakes, have perspective when things don't go our way, and relinquish control when we have done everything we could do. The fact that you have read this book, or even picked up a parenting book, is a testament to your desire to love your children and to be a better parent. I applaud you in your desires and, from one parent to another, I am grateful for the good parents of the world who are strengthening their homes and children. It is my sincerest belief that originating from home individuals, societies, and countries are strengthened.

Sincerely,

Katie.

About Kharis Publishing:

Kharis Publishing, an imprint of Kharis Media LLC, is a leading Christian and inspirational book publisher based in Aurora, Chicago metropolitan area, Illinois. Kharis' dual mission is to give voice to under-represented writers (including women and first-time authors) and equip orphans in developing countries with literacy tools. That is why, for each book sold, the publisher channels some of the proceeds into providing books and computers for orphanages in developing countries so that these kids may learn to read, dream, and grow. For a limited time, Kharis Publishing is accepting unsolicited queries for nonfiction (Christian, self-help, memoirs, business, health and wellness) from qualified leaders, professionals, pastors, and ministers. Learn more at: https://kharispublishing.com/